PHENOMENOLOGICAL ETHICS

PHENOMENOLOGICAL ETHICS

An Introduction

BENULAL DHAR

RAWAT PUBLICATIONS

Jaipur • New Delhi • Bangalore • Mumbai • Hyderabad • Guwahati

ISBN 81-316-0193-5

Published by
Prem Rawat for **Rawat Publications**
Satyam Apts, Sector 3, Jawahar Nagar, Jaipur 302 004 (India)
Phone: 0141 265 1748 / 7006 Fax: 0141 265 1748
E-mail: info@rawatbooks.com
Website: www.rawatbooks.com

New Delhi Office
4858/24, Ansari Road, Daryaganj, New Delhi 110 002
Phone: 011 2326 3290

Also at Bangalore, Mumbai, Hyderabad and Guwahati

Typeset by Rawat Computers, Jaipur

To
the Memory of
my Mother
Smt. Priyodabala Dhar

and

my Mother-in-law
Smt. Anjali Biswas

Contents

	Foreword	9
	Preface	11
1	Introduction	15
2	Moore's Intuitionism and the Phenomenological Value-Ethics	32
3	Hartmann's Critique of Kant's Ethical Framework	48
4	Kant's Ethical Framework: Scheler's Phenomenological Critique	59
5	Hartmann's Value-Platonism	75
6	Scheler's Value-Ethics	98
7	Experiencing Values	128
8	Value-perspectivism: A Critique	145
9	Some Concluding Remarks	150
	Bibliography	172
	Index	178

Foreword

While Husserl's phenomenological philosophy brings to bear a new perspective on issues relating to meaning and apriorism, he also seems to have influenced Hartmann and Scheler – the two outstanding philosophers outside the twentieth century world of English-speaking philosophers – to think about moral values and ethical ideas closely along phenomenological lines. Both these philosophers develop a critique of Kantian formalistic ethics that is significant in itself. Their major thrust towards phenomenological grasping of values by direct and immediate intuition comes through as quite opposed to Kantian formalism.

Dr Benulal Dhar has attempted a comprehensive exposition of the ethical ideas developed by Hartmann and Scheler against the background of Kant's rational formalism. That sensing of values directly by intuition always precedes the moral judgement is the corner-stone of phenomenological ethics as worked out by Hartmann and Scheler. For the phenomenologists, the domain of values is autonomous and independent of the cognizing consciousness; values are ideals, and are not quite like spatio-temporal objects. Again, the grasping of values takes place through emotion rather than reason, a feature that generally characterizes phenomenological approach to values.

It is heartening to note that Dr Benulal Dhar goes on to deal with these matters and their subtle nuances by means of perceptive analysis that brings out the insights into value-ethics. His effort to bring together the basic ideas of phenomenological ethics with pointed clarity and lucid style of expression is highly commendable and deserves due recognition.

To my mind, Dr Benulal Dhar has done a signal service by bringing out this book which will go a long way in enriching philosophical perspective of the present-day reader. In the Indian context, the book will be a welcome addition to a very small corpus of works on phenomenological ethics.

Ranjan K. Ghosh

Preface

Phenomenological philosophy as developed by Husserl has provided a germinating ground for the growth of ideas in various disciplines, and ethics is one of them. The value-ethics of Nicolai Hartmann and Max Scheler are developed under the general influence of phenomenology. Though Hartmann is known basically as a Platonic thinker, yet he remains indebted to phenomenology to a great extent in erecting the edifice of his value-ethics. Scheler, on the other hand, formulates his value-ethics directly on the basis of phenomenological ideas. Besides, their ethical theories themselves are considered to be major attempts in the field of values in the twentieth century. The influences that have contributed to the development of these two ethical theories are not unilateral but multilateral in nature though the pre-dominant one is that of phenomenology. And it is in the spirit of their phenomenological approach that we shall study them in the following pages.

Some of the problems to be addressed within this study would include: (a) What is the nature of values? (b) How are they experienced? (c) In what sense, values are perspectival and relative? (d) What is the meaning of *a priori* from a phenomenological standpoint, and in what sense phenomenological ethics could be called *a priori* ethics?

The entire book is divided into nine chapters: *Chapter I* not only introduces the subject-matter of this study, but also deals with at some length the various aspects of Husserl's phenomenological method under the influence of which these two ethical theories developed. *Chapter II* deals with some affinities of

Moore's intuitionism with the views of Hartmann and Scheler. This chapter is of exploratory in our search for some useful insights, which may have some bearing on our central inquiry. *Chapters III* and *IV* centre on a phenomenological critique of Kant's ethical framework by Hartmann and Scheler, respectively. This should provide a springboard for a more sympathetic understanding of what is called "material" ethics of Hartmann and Scheler. *Chapters V* and *VI* are devoted to the basic issues underlying their value-ethics, though neither of them is treated as a "historical" thinker. *Chapter VII* makes an attempt to answer the question: How values are experienced? *Chapter VIII* would offer a critical account of what is value-perspectivism in the ethical theories of Hartmann and Scheler. What do they mean by speaking of "perceiving" values, while meticulously safe-guarding their position of value-absolutism, is the question that will engage us in this chapter. And in the concluding *Chapter IX*, some general insights will be gleaned from the maze of details that have gone into this study.

The origin of this work goes back to my doctoral days at the University of North Bengal nearly fifteen years ago. After receiving my doctoral degree I continued to work on phenomenological ethics in the light of the views of Hartmann and Scheler to bring it to the present form. Meanwhile, I also benefited immensely from the discussions I earlier had with some of the leading phenomenological thinkers during my visit to Tuebingen University (Germany) and other leading phenomenological centres in Europe on a scholarship I received under the Indo-German Cultural Exchange Programme.

I owe several debts of gratitude. At the outset, I would like to express my deep and profound gratitude to my teacher Dr Ranjan K. Ghosh, presently, Senior Fellow, Indian Council of Philosophical Research, whose critical comments and insightful discussions at every stage of the work were very fruitful and encouraging. He graciously gave of his time to go through all the chapters of this work and made a lot of possible improvements. However, for the inadequacies that still remain, I alone am responsible. I also record here my gratefulness to him for having readily agreed to write the "Foreword" for this book. Again, it was he who for the first time brought to my notice the significant convergence of the insights of Moore and the phenomenological thinkers in a particular respect.

I am extremely grateful to Late Professor Klaus Hartmann, Philosophisches Seminar, Tuebingen University, Germany with whom I had the opportunity to discuss several issues that I have dealt within the present study. I consider myself to be singularly fortunate in having had the occasion to read with him several portions of phenomenological texts. I also carry the vivid memories of my discussions with many of the other philosophers especially Dr Klaus Bort and Dr Dietmar Koch, who took great pains in explaining some of the difficult phenomenological ideas. For this I remain ever thankful to them.

I gratefully acknowledge the help received from Professor Eva H. Cadwallader, Westminster College, New Wilmington, U.S.A., Professor Eugene Kelly, New York Institute of Technology, New York, U.S.A. and Professor Philip Blosser, Lenoir-Rhyne College, North Carolina, U.S.A., who were kind enough to send me copies of their books as also a number of their published articles addressed to the philosophies of Hartmann and Scheler.

I record here my gratefulness to Professor Ram Adhar Mall, (Germany) with whom I discussed some points relating to this study and also to Professor Kalyan Bagchi, Visvabharati, whose lectures on Kant's philosophy helped me a lot. I avail myself of this opportunity to express my gratitude to my teacher, Professor Ranjit Kr. Acharjee, Department of Philosophy, Ramkrishna Mahavidyalaya, (Tripura University), Professor Madhabendra Nath Mitra, Department of Philosophy, Jadavpur University, and Professor Dilip Kr. Mohanta, Department of Philosophy, Calcutta University, who have been sources of encouragement and support. I am thankful to my teachers and the friends, Department of Philosophy, University of North Bengal, and to Professor Niranjan Ch. Paul, formerly Principal, Sukanta Mahavidyalaya and Dr Mukul Nath, the present Principal, Sukanta Mahavidyalaya for kind support. I also thank all my colleagues at Sukanta Mahavidyalaya, for their friendship over the years.

Thanks are also due to the Editor of *Indian Philosophical Quarterly* for permitting me to draw from two of my articles published in volume XXX, No. 2, (2001) and volume XXVI, No. 2, (1999) and to Editor of *The Journal of the Indian Academy of*

Philosophy for the use of my article published in volume XL, No. 1 & 2, (2001).

I am indebted to the following institutions: (i) North Bengal University Library, (ii) Indian Council of Philosophical Research Library, Lucknow, (iii) Philosophisches Seminar Library and Central Library, Tuebingen University, Germany, (iv) Husserl Archives, Freiburg and Koln Universities, Germany, (v) Indian Institute of Advanced Study, Shimla, (vi) Reference Library, Delhi University and Punjab University Library, Chandigarh.

My friends Sarvashri Jatishwar Bharati, Sanjib Das and Shusanta Modak have helped me in various ways in the preparation of the typescript of the book. Thanks are also due to Shri Pranit Rawat of Rawat Publications for evincing interest in the work and undertaking its publication.

Finally, I am also deeply grateful to my wife, Rekha, for her untiring care and moral support in all matters. The innocent look of my two dear children, Rajarshi and Shreosee and their radiating cheer remained an eloquent and unfailing source of encouragement.

B.L. Dhar

1

Introduction

I

When we look back on the broad conspectus of the ethical ideas and theories that have been studied and pursued by academic philosophers in the English-speaking countries during the century that has just drawn to a close, we find an overwhelming preoccupation with the views mainly of English-speaking philosophers and thinkers. This has, of course, been duly acknowledged by some thinkers and writers on ethical philosophy sometime even with an apologia such as, for example, one finds in the book *Twentieth Century Ethics*. Hancock in his introduction to the book is clearly conscious of this "limitation" as he remarks, "that, unfortunate as it may be, work in ethical theory in the English-speaking countries in recent times has been done independently of work outside these areas."[1] He hastens to add,

> No suggestion is being made that the work of Nicolai Hartmann or Max Scheler, for example, is less important than the work of, say, G.E. Moore or Charles Stevenson. The suggestion is simply that the recent work of English-speaking philosophers is in some important sense autonomous and can therefore be treated in a book such as this by itself.[2]

The above-quoted remarks help us to set the perspective for the present work. That there is a lamentable lack of proper exposure to the tradition outside of what goes on within the English-speaking world, insofar as ethical philosophy is concerned, would be commonly shared by many a present-day scholar even if sometimes pricked by the prefatory remarks, such as, one finds in Hancock's book. A serious attempt, in our view, is called for in order to remedy the situation by investigating another dominant philosophical trend that has been carried out in the West, namely, the phenomenological philosophy. The present work proposes to move in this direction.

Phenomenological philosophy as a systematic movement came into focus with the writings of Edmund Husserl, with the publication of his *Logical Investigations* in 1901. It was more a "movement" than a set of doctrines. For, it was diffused by many thinkers and writers in Germany, France and in many other countries in Europe and America after the tradition was inaugurated by Husserl. And as a movement, it occupied itself mainly with philosophical methodology and epistemological issues. That Husserl is said to have been interested in ethical philosophy as well, has been widely acclaimed by many phenomenological thinkers. As Marvin Farber, a student of Husserl, writes,

> In the writings published during his lifetime, Husserl showed that he also had in mind the experience and nature of values, and what he stated indicates the direction of his ethical thought. The ethical manuscripts left at his death give a greater indication of his conception of the phenomenology of values ... . Husserl's serious interest in ethics is shown by the number of times he elected to give lectures and seminars on that subject.[3]

However, we have chosen to deal in the present work with two important continental thinkers, namely, Nicolai Hartmann and Max Scheler who have paid exclusive attention to the theory of values, in general, and moral values, in particular, of course within the broad framework of phenomenological thinking. Nicolai Hartmann (1882–1950) was born in Riga, Latvia and began his academic career with intensive work on Greek philosophy under the supervision of Hermann Cohen and Paul Natorp at Marburg in Germany. His monumental work *Ethics* first appeared in German in 1926, and an English translation in 1932. The ethical theory expounded in this book seems to contain three broad aspects:[4] (i) Metaphysical or Platonism, (ii) phenomenological, and (iii) aretaic aspect. It may be said at the outset that he cherishes great respect for Plato throughout his life and this is evident from the following statement. He writes,

> ... Platonic ideal is not dead, the ideal of ruling and moulding mankind spiritually through the power of philosophical perception, through the vision of Ideas.[5]

However, his interest does not lie with Plato's metaphysics in general, but with the idea of Being. For, he equates the being of values with the being of Ideas.

With regard to the second dimension of his ethical thought, it may be pointed out that whether Hartmann is a member of the phenomenological movement or not is not beyond dispute. But he is certainly, to some extent, influenced by Husserl's phenomenology. His philosophy contains considerable amount of phenomenological ingredients, though this phenomenology is his own. Hartmann is not concerned with foundational issues of phenomenology but uses it as far as it is of help in dealing with the philosophical problems and issues. So phenomenology comes to his use only when he employs it as a part of his method to deal with philosophical problems. As for him, any reflections on method bear meaning only when it succeeds in resolving the philosophical problems and issues. In ethics, he uses phenomenology when he discusses particularly the way in which values are discovered, though he does not affix any label to this procedure as phenomenological. As Spiegelberg says,

> Hartman thus subscribes to the familiar intuition of essences (*Wesensschau*) in the sense of the phenomenologists as an essential part of his own phenomenological method. It is exemplified all through Hartmann's writings.[6]

Besides, Hartmann recognizes the legitimate role of "feeling" in the discovery of values. It is taken by him, like Scheler, to have cognitive authority. It is an emotional mode of cognition, which is underived from reason or rationality. It is non-logical yet primal form of value-cognition. In describing this mode of emotive cognition of values, Hartmann has recourse to the phenomenological notion of *intuition*. He affirms with Husserl that there are universal essences, which are "ideal" in nature, though their beings do not originate from thought. He acknowledges Scheler's use of phenomenology to refute Kantian formalism. In fact, Husserl and Scheler exert great influence on the development of Hartmann's theory of ethics.

Now for the aretaic aspect, the basis of ethical evaluation is character or disposition of an agent. Such a theory places virtue rather than the good or the right at its centre. Aristotle first presented such a theory, and Hartmann is definitely influenced by Aristotle in reinterpreting the virtues in the light of modern European ethos. By "virtue", Hartman seems to understand a "dispositional property" exhibited by a moral agent in order to actualize an ideal value that subsists in a trans-natural realm. Thus, for Hartmann, each virtue is always associated with an ideal value.

Finally, and importantly, Hartmann's is an exercise in independent and rigorous thinking enlivened by exceptional quality of his writings. One seldom finds quotations from other philosophical writings, except occasional references to and criticisms of other's points of view. In addition, one finds thoroughness and systematic presentation of thought in his *Ethics*.

Max Scheler (1874–1928) was born in Munich, and began his academic career with a doctorate received from Jena University. He was basically an independent thinker who at some times developed and used phenomenology in his own way to analyse such issues as moral values, religion, emotions, etc. He develops a value-ethics in his *Formalism in Ethics and Non-formal Ethics of Values* (1913/16) which is primarily based on Husserlian phenomenology. This work is considered to be a pioneering undertaking in applied phenomenology. However, he does not feel bound by Husserl's detailed phenomenological programme. He takes phenomenology as an attitude or a "way of viewing" and develops an unorthodox interpretation of Husserl apropos of his own purposes. He is said to have met Husserl at a party at Halle in 1901, and immensely benefited from a conversation with him. Though Scheler differs from Husserl on many points in his later life, he remained convinced of Husserl's view that a philosopher must keep himself off from all kinds of *presuppositions* while philosophizing and rely on the evidence of non-sensible intuition alone. Along with Husserl's ideal of a presuppositionless philosophy and the notion of "categorial intuition" as developed by him in his *Logical Investigations*, Scheler also endorses former's doctrine of "ideal objects". These Husserlian conceptions ultimately pave the way for Scheler's theory of values. Scheler also applies phenomenology to another field which remains outside of Husserl's area of interest, that is, the field of emotions. He rejects the primacy of logical reasoning favoured by Husserl, and attempts at an elaborate phenomenology of feeling as a mode of value-apprehension. The significance of Scheler's advocacy of phenomenological thinking has been brought out by John R. Staude in the following manner:

> Thus, Scheler's phenomenology not only represented a repudiation of scientific rationalism; it was intended to counteract modern man's tendency to filter his experience through abstract conceptual structures. In this sense, it required what Scheler called "a continuous *de-symbolization* of the world," forcing man to return to the immediacy of his experience prior to its symbolisation and conceptualisation.[7]

Besides Husserl, Scheler draws inspiration from the writings of Pascal, Bergson and Brentano for the development of his ethical thought. He declares, following Pascal, that the heart has its own logic, which it does not borrow from the logic of the mind. In addition, the same point is stressed by Bergson too. According to John R. Staude, Scheler

> agreed with Bergson that intellectualization alienated man from Being. The hard cold stare of the impersonal intellect, motivated by the will to power, could grasp only the external contours of being. To discover the inscape of things – to use Hopkins' lovely phrase – Scheler became convinced that the philosopher must purify himself of whatever selfish designs he might harbor in his heart. With Plato, Scheler discovered that philosophy begins in *wonder*.[8]

As regards Brentano's influence, it is said that Scheler's theory of cognitive emotion and its application in the realm of values are directly borrowed from Brentano's writings. As Calhoun and Solomon write,

> Scheler's monumental reconstruction of our idea of emotion grew directly out of Franz Brentano's work. Both construct intentional theories of emotion; both wrestle with the relation between emotion and our knowledge of values; and both *elevate emotion to a place of prominence* in what might loosely be called the intellectual life.[9]

However, Scheler distinguishes his own point of view from Brentano's by saying that (i) values are distinct from emotions and (ii) some emotions, not all, are intentional in character.

It is of some significance that both Hartman and Scheler, more Scheler perhaps than Hartmann, have delved deep into Kant's ethical views as they develop specific and pointed arguments against Kant's formal apriorism. Hartmann devotes a section of his *Ethics* exclusively to critically evaluate Kant's ethical framework and develops a "material" ethics as against Kant's formal ethics. However, in Scheler's ethics, we find a continual reference to Kant. He makes a thorough critical examination of the basic structure of Kantian formal ethics and develops, like Hartmann, a "material" ethics of value. But through their criticisms of Kant, both Hartmann and Scheler recognize the greatness and profundity of Kant's ethical ideas and identify some points in Kant's ethics, which can be kept intact within the idea of a non-formal ethics of value as well. Thus, in Scheler's *magnum opus* three philosophical interests coincide: phenomenology, Kantianism and value-ethics.

Though our aim in the present venture is not to make a comparative study of Hartmann and Scheler, yet the relationship between them deserves a mention. Hartmann is a junior contemporary of Scheler. Both of them mention each other and point out the similarities and differences of views on some matters of ethical concern, though in a marginal way. Hartmann in his preface to his book *Ethics* expresses solidarity with Scheler to establish a "material" ethics of value in opposition to Kant's formal apriorism. On some points of his critique of Kant, Hartmann directly acknowledges Scheler's points of criticism against Kant's ethics. As Spiegelberg says,

> Hartmann's contacts with Max Scheler were much closer. Scheler's ethical writings had been Hartmann's point of

> departure in the development of his own *Ethik*. So when Hartmann joined him at the University of Cologne in 1925 hardly without Scheler's active support, their connections became even more direct and intense.[10]

On the other hand, Scheler, in his preface to the third edition of *Formalism in Ethics*, mentions Hartmann and expresses his own views on some points of Hartmann's philosophy.

Now, for undertaking any systematic investigation, it is sometimes helpful to cast the net wide and far. Such a move would be inspired by the hope that various ideas may be gleaned from the sources that are not accredited as phenomenological. A thinker such as G.E. Moore, who is readily considered to be belonging to the British tradition of analytic philosophy, provides an important clue to our understanding of the phenomenological idea of the critique of naturalism. As Marvin Farber points out,

> With no apparent conscious motivation, a writer like G.E. Moore appears to point to an impasse to naturalism in ethics, and to be trying to achieve what idealists in Germany had wanted to accomplish in more elaborate ways.[11]

Not only this, Scheler, a thoroughgoing phenomenological ethicist, finds Moore's ethical views to be similar to that of his own. One can also trace similar points of convergence between Moore and the phenomenological ethicists through Moore's favourable review of Franz Brentano's *The Origin of the Knowledge of Right and Wrong* in *The International Journal of Ethics* Vol. 14 (1903). In the present work, we have ventured to spell out some points of similarities on ethical views of both Moore and Scheler. We have also discussed some points of affinities between Moore's theory of good and Hartmann's theory of value as brought out by Cadwallader in her book, *Searchlight on Values*.

II

Both Hartmann and Scheler have worked out their value-ethics based partially or wholly on the spirit of phenomenology. Hartmann, though avowedly a value-Platonist, looks for a moral epistemology founded on the basis of phenomenological insights.

Scheler, on the other hand, seeks to erect his ethical edifice on phenomenological principles. These two thinkers have used the phenomenological tools and techniques not in their orthodox form, but in their own ways to suit their specific purposes. So in order to sharpen the focus clearly on the ethical writings of Hartmann and Scheler, it may be quite helpful to discuss the cardinal principles of phenomenological methodology in brief as formulated by Edmund Husserl.

The *first* and basic methodological principle of philosophy, according to Husserl, is that it must eschew all presuppositions. In paragraph 63 of his *Ideas I*, Husserl says: "... it (phenomenology) therefore demands the completest freedom from all assumptions."[12] According to this ideal, one cannot assume anything or take anything for granted unless there are proper reasons for it. Our acts of thought refer to external or even non-existent and fictitious objects. However, the assertions concerning the existence or non-existence of these objects cannot be assumed to be true when one is engaged in philosophizing. The physical and psychological realities that transcend consciousness cannot be taken for granted. A true philosophical discipline is not at all concerned with the question relating to the existence or non-existence of physical and psychical realities. Rather, it must remain indifferent to them. According to Marvin Farber,

> There is no assertion concerning real existence, and hence no use can be made of premises drawn from metaphysics or natural science, especially psychology. It is this metaphysical, natural-scientific, and psychological freedom from presuppositions, *and no other kind*, that Husserl proposed to realize at this time.[13]

The reason behind adopting this ideal of presuppositionlessness as his methodological requirement is that Husserl aims at founding philosophy as what he calls "rigorous" science, which would provide us with "pure and absolute knowledge". By "rigorous" Husserl means that which does not take anything dogmatically without giving sufficient reasons for it. According to Husserl, the method of philosophy is to be "radical" in the sense that it does not take for granted any assumptions, beliefs, etc. regarding the existence of physical and psychical things. Even the physical existence and psychical faculties of one who is philosophizing cannot be presupposed. For, if once anything is presupposed dogmatically, when one has to build up a system of "scientific" philosophy, then there is a possibility of the philosophy to turn out to be dogmatic, which cannot provide pure and scientific knowledge. The *hidden* presuppositions may vitiate the whole enterprise of philosophy, and as a result, the conclusions drawn by such philosophy may collapse into nothing.

In fact, Husserl wants to establish philosophy on the basis of "unimpeachable rationality", which must be *rigorous* from its very starting-point. And this project can be fulfilled, Husserl realizes, only by the rigid application of phenomenological method having "scientific" rigour of being presuppositionless. For Husserl, "to be presuppositionsless" and "to be certain" are synonymous expressions. The basic spirit of a "rigorous" science – the Husserlian designation for philosophy – is that one must proceed towards establishing a source of apodictic knowledge by thoroughly and systematically examining all the naïve beliefs and prejudices and thus nothing is left, which is open to doubt.

Secondly, the natural attitude for Husserl is clearly not a philosophical attitude at all. Philosophical attitude must take leave of the natural attitude and it is the technique of reduction, which makes it possible. Husserl therefore develops his theory of reduction on the basis of radical criticism of the "natural attitude". The phenomenological reduction eliminates the "general thesis" of the natural standpoint as such. He who philosophizes must have to take a radical attitude, which consists in disregarding the presuppositions of a world existing independently of us. He would require suspending the judgements, which consist of certain commonly held beliefs and prejudices regarding the natural world, to lay the foundation of a "scientific" philosophy. Husserl writes,

> Again, I may freely abstain from entertaining any belief about experience – which I did. This simply means that I refuse to assert the reality of the world … . I must similarly abstain from any other of my opinions, judgments, and valuations about the world, since these likewise assume the reality of the world. But for these, as for other phenomena, epistemological abstention

> does not mean their disappearance, at least not as pure phenomena.[14]

To describe this attitude, Husserl uses the Greek term "epoche", which is used by Greek sceptics to refer to a suspension of judgment. Being a mathematician, Husserl also identifies the basic meaning of reduction with the mathematical operation of "*bracketing*". The underlying idea of this metaphor is that a philosopher should detach or dissociate himself from the context of his naïve or natural living. A mathematician parenthesizes a mathematical equation, not in order to eliminate it, but to put it out of question for the time being in order to concentrate on the larger context of the equation. Likewise, a philosopher must have to "put out of action" all one's presuppositions by placing them in "brackets" while engaged in philosophical activity in order to concentrate on the "object" of investigation.

Thus, the first and foremost fundamental aspect of this technique of reduction is negative. It seeks to put the "natural attitude" into brackets, and this does not in any way mean denying it. Nor does it mean transforming it into anti-thesis, doubt or indecision. By putting it into brackets, a philosopher rather keeps his way of philosophizing free from the influence of "naturalistic thesis". With the performance of the *epoche* what a philosopher arrives at is the region of "*pure*" phenomena or essences. As Herbert Spiegelberg rightly says:

> Reduction is not merely a moving away from the natural world but a moving towards something ... . The goal of this movement is none other than transcendental subjectivity.[15]

Thirdly, the operation of phenomenological reduction opens up the region of pure consciousness. According to Husserl, consciousness can be understood only in terms of its acts and these acts of consciousness are *intentional* in character. In his earlier writings, intentionality is held by Husserl to be the characteristic feature of consciousness, but in his later writings, he understands it as the very *essence* of consciousness. In his *The Paris Lectures* he says, "*The essence of consciousness, in which I live as my own self, is the so-called intentionality*. Consciousness is always consciousness of something."[16]

The term "intentionality" has been borrowed by Husserl from Brentano, who provides a psychological interpretation of it. For Brentano, psychical phenomena can be distinguished from the physical phenomena by the fact that the former, unlike the latter, are characterized by "intentional relation" or by what he calls "intentional inexistence" of the intended object. However, Husserl, being a staunch opponent of psychologism, rejects Brentano's psychological interpretation and salvages the concept from psychologism by giving it a transcendental interpretation.

Again Husserl writes, "We understood under Intentionality the unique peculiarity of experiences 'to be consciousness *of* something'."[17] The pure consciousness that is stripped of all contingency and accidental characteristics, according to Husserl, can be understood only in terms of acts which are referential in character. And this applies not merely to our cognitive states but also to states of feeling, desiring, valuing, wishing and so on. The acts of consciousness have been termed in *Ideas I* as "noetic act" or "noesis". These are not to be confused with psychological acts which occur in time and refer to physical or mental objects. These intentional acts are directed towards their intentional correlate, namely, "noema" or "noematic content". Noema is *sinn* or sense. It is the immediate object of perceiving, judging, etc. Noema is not itself the object towards which the act of consciousness is directed. Rather, noema is "the object as it is intended" or meant.

Fourthly, keeping in view our context, let us analyse the nature of phenomenological intuition which would clarify as well as supplement our discussion so far. Phenomenology has been described by Husserl as "a pure descriptive discipline which studies the whole field of transcendental consciousness in the light of pure intuition."[18] It is considered to be an "eidetic" science or what Husserl calls the "science of pure phenomena", which describes the pure phenomena as they appear in pure consciousness.

Now, what are the essences or phenomena? The Greek term "*eidos*" is meant by Husserl the essence of what a thing is. Here the term "essence" is not to be understood exactly in Platonic sense in which they are "other-worldly" objects. They are also not to be regarded as identical with what Kant means by "phenomena". For Kant, phenomena are smokescreens, which conceal "noumena" or "things-in-themselves". However, for Husserl, phenomena are something, which "show" themselves in the mode of givenness. Nothing lies behind it. All phenomena whether they are experienced, contemplated or fantasized alike are stripped off all kinds of existential or metaphysical references. However, what is remarkable in the idea of essence is that it has for Husserl the status of an object, which can only be grasped through "eidetic intuition" as an unerring source of rational understanding.

After the operation of reduction, what is immediately revealed to a phenomenologist is the field of "pure phenomena" or what Husserl calls "the domain of the absolutely given" which awaits description and clarification. The pure phenomena or essences reside in the immanent region of pure consciousness, which is generally, according to Husserl, the necessary characteristic of cognition. In the case of natural cognition, the object exists in space and time as transcendent object and it cannot be the part of cognitive process. This is known as the problem of transcendence in epistemology. Husserl marks this as a "riddle that stands in the path of cognition of the natural sort and is the incentive for new investigations."[19] And because of this problem of transcendence, that natural cognition, according to Husserl, bears the mark of being questionable. "We do not understand", Husserl writes,

> how perception can reach transcendent objects, but we understand how perception can reach the immanent, provided it is reflective and purely immanent perception which has undergone reduction.[20]

That is, unlike natural cognition, in pure intuition, object can very well be the part of cognitive process. Because, pure essences, which are objects of immanent perception, reside in the immanent region of consciousness. Further, in natural cognition, what is intended is *not* "given" as the object of cognition exists in spatio-temporal world. But in the case of *pure* cognition, what is intended is "given" in the strictest sense of the term. Because, in this case the "object" resides in the consciousness as "absolutely immanent data". Furthermore, in phenomenological intuition, pure phenomena are given *immanently* and directly to pure consciousness. This immediate and direct givenness of pure essences dispels all doubts. "This givenness", Husserl writes,

> which rules out any meaningful doubt, consists of a simply immediate "seeing" and apprehending of the intended object itself as it is, and it constitutes the precise concept of evidence (Evidenz) understood as immediate evidence.[21]

Needless to mention, in phenomenological intuition "objects" are given and grasped without recourse to any concept, symbol, sign, instruction, etc. It is the intentional acts of pure consciousness, a radical attitude, and a new way of looking at "things", which enables us to gain an *a priori* and direct insight into the pure essences. Thus, the phenomenological intuition makes it possible for a phenomenologist to go immediately and directly to the domain of pure essences to have signification independently of any explanation – whether psychological or metaphysical. Here lies the significance of Husserl's slogan: "Back to things themselves". Husserl summarizes his point with regard to the nature of phenomenological intuition in the following way:

> Actually, therefore, phenomenological explication is nothing like "metaphysical construction"; and it is neither overtly nor covertly a theorizing with adopted presuppositions or helpful thoughts drawn from the historical metaphysical tradition. It stands in sharpest contrast to all that, because it proceeds within the limits of pure "intuition," or rather of pure sense-explication based on a fulfilling givenness of the sense itself .... Phenomenological explication does nothing but *explicate the sense the world has for us all, prior to any philosophizing* ...[22]

Fifthly, unlike analytic philosophers, who are content with the analysis of concepts and language and their logical structures, Husserl is concerned with intentional analysis of essential structure of experience, which is made possible with*out* linguistic expressions, symbols or signs. In fact, phenomenology (at least primarily) is not concerned with language. For, pure intuition needs no language but only an attitude. As Husserl says,

> In the epoch of vigorous reaction against Scholasticism the war cry was: "Away with empty word analyses! We must question things themselves. Back to experience, to seeing, which alone

> can give to our words sense and rational justification." Very much to the point.[23]

Human beings do not use language as a ready-made tool for inter-personal communication, which is independent of his experiential acts. Unlike analytic philosophers, according to whom speech-act is a kind of rule-governed behaviour, Husserl thinks that speech-act is an intentional *act* of consciousness and the meaning arises out of the noesis-noema correlation. Therefore, meaning does not reside primarily in the linguistic expression but in the noetic acts of consciousness. Husserl's position in this regard has clearly been brought out by Edo Pivcevic as follows:

> His position is that concepts are types of meaning and meanings are not simply kinds of linguistic skill. They presuppose certain *acts of meaning*. In particular, references to conceptual meanings presuppose the ability of apprehending meanings as ideal unities in acts of reflection. There are (he would argue) no conceptual meanings *per se* in abstraction from such acts.[24]

And *lastly*, let us now turn to Husserl's notion of categorial intuition "that ultimately opened the way for Scheler's theory of value, which is clearly based on the phenomenological notions of 'intuition of essences' (Wesensschau) and the 'material a priori.'"[25] Husserl recognizes the obvious fact that a particular, say, a shade of colour on the surface of a thing is an individual shade. Appearance of the colour red on the flag or in the blood is the case of individual shade of species red and these individual shades are directly known by sight, though the species red is not a direct object of our sight. Thus, there can be two ways of attending to such a situation: (i) it is possible to have a direct awareness of the individual red shade through our senses (here, sight) as also, (ii) it is possible to apprehend species red or red as such through intuition. Husserl puts the matter as follows.

> But the same appearance sustains different acts in the two cases. In the first case it provides the presentative basis for an act of *individual* reference, i.e. for an act in which we apply ourselves to the apparent thing itself, and "mean" this thing or this feature, this part of the thing. In the latter case it provides the

> presentative basis for an act of conception and reference directed to a Species: i.e. while the thing appears, or rather the feature in the thing, it is not this objective feature, this feature here and now, that we mean. We mean its *content*, its "Idea; ' we mean, not this aspect of red in the house, but Red as such.[26]

The point is that though our gaze is directed towards the individual red shade, we intend or mean the red as such in intuition. This has readily been acknowledged by Husserl thus:

> ... the act in which we mean the Species, is in fact essentially different from the act in which we mean the individual, whether, in this later case, we refer to a whole concrete thing, or to an individual piece or property attaching to it.[27]

Further, on Husserl's theory, species red can be the "object" of an act and is given differently from how the individual red shade is given to our apprehension. While directing our attention towards the individual shade, we "mean" or "intend" the species red and thereby species red acquires the status of an object. In Husserl's own words,

> While the red object and its emphasized aspect of red appear before us, we are rather "meaning" the single identical Red, and are meaning it in a novel conscious *manner*, though which precisely the Species, and not the individual, becomes our object.[28]

Furthermore, for Husserl, there are two types of objects – real and ideal. Real is defined in terms of temporality. For example, a pen or a present state of mind exists in certain duration of time. However, temporality does not belong to what is ideal. According to Husserl, reality is defined in terms of temporality but not what is ideal. For, the being of the ideal is timeless. In case of colour, the individual shade of, say, red is temporal, existing on the surface of an object, and therefore, is real. But the species red is timeless and therefore, ideal. It must be noted that what is ideal is neither spatio-temporal nor fictitious or non-sensical but something that exists as "genuine object". In short, the categorical intuition is meant to be an immediate and non-sensuous insight into species, genus or for that matter, a *universal* object. It is a new mode of apprehension, which constitutes the intuitive presence of the universal object, like species red.

Now, at this stage, some reflections on the foregoing accounts and analyses are called for. The phenomenological method has been introduced and developed by Husserl in order to put forward a programme for radical reform in philosophy. It is a radical method for philosophical investigation, which has the scientific rigour of its own. One of the basic but teachable parts of phenomenological method is that philosophy must be free from all presuppositions or preconceptions which have not been thoroughly examined. In order to eliminate all our naïve beliefs and prejudices in the existence of the natural world and metaphysical entity, Husserl introduces the technique of phenomenological reduction. It helps us to leave behind our whole host of presuppositions, beliefs and the theories of different kinds, and facilitates a philosopher to concentrate on the essential data of knowing consciousness. The latter is an original form of intuition, which apprehends its object "in person" without the mediation of anything else. And this is the core of Husserl's phenomenological method, which exerted a great influence upon the ethical theories of Scheler and Hartmann.

Notes

1. Hancock, R.N. *Twentieth Century Ethics*, (Columbia University Press, 1974), pp. 1-2.
2. Ibid., p. 2.
3. Farber, M. *Phenomenology and Existence,* (Harper & Row Publisher, New York, 1967), pp. 185-86.
4. Cadwallader, E.H. *Searchlight on Values*, (University Press of America, Lanham, 1984), p. 46.
5. Hartmann, N. *Ethics,* (George Allen & Unwin Ltd., London, 1967), Third Impression, p. 94.
6. Spiegelberg, H. *The Phenomenological Movement: A Historical Introduction*, (Martinus Nijhoff, The Hague, 1971), 2nd edition, Vol. 1, p. 377.
7. Staude, J.R. *Max Scheler: An Intellectual Portrait*, (The Free Press, New York, 1967), p. 22.
8. Ibid., p. 21.

9. Calhoun, C. and Solomon, R.C. "What is an Emotion"? *Classic Readings in Philosophical Psychology,* (Oxford University Press, Oxford, 1984), p. 218. (our emphases).
10. Spiegelberg, H. *The Phenomenological Movement,* op. cit. p. 359.
11. Farber, M. *Phenomenology and Existence*, op. cit. p. 166.
12. Husserl, E. *Ideas I,* Translated by W.R. Boyce Gibson, (George Allen and Unwin Ltd., London, 1969), 5th Impression, p. 188.
13. Farber, M. *The Aims of Phenomenology,* (Harper Torch Books, New York, 1966), p. 32.
14. Husserl, E. *The Paris Lectures,* Translated by P. Koestenbaum, (Martinus Nijhoff, The Hague, 1975), 2nd Edition, pp. 7-8.
15. Spiegelberg, H. *The Phenomenological Movement*, Vol. 1, op. cit. p. 136.
16. Husserl, E. *The Paris Lectures*, op. cit. p. 12.
17. Husserl, E. *Ideas I*, op. cit. p. 242.
18. Ibid., p. 176.
19. Husserl, E. *The Idea of Phenomenology,* Translated by W.P. Alston and G. Nakhnikian, (Martinus Nijhoff, The Hague, 1964), p. 28.
20. Ibid., p. 39.
21. Ibid., p. 28.
22. Husserl, E.*Cartesian Meditations: An Introduction to Phenomenology,* Translated by Darion Cairns, (Martinus Nijhoff, The Hague, 1960), pp. 150-51.
23. Husserl, E. "Philosophy as Rigorous Science", *Phenomenology and the Crisis of Philosophy,* Translated by Quentin Lauer, (Harper & Row Publisher, New York, 1965), pp. 96-97.
24. Pivcevic, E. "Concepts, Phenomenology and Philosophical Understanding", in Edo Pivcevic (ed.), *Phenomenology and Philosophical Understanding,* (Cambridge University Press, Cambridge, 1975), p. 284.
25. Blosser, P. "Ethics in Scheler", in Lester Embree and Others (ed.), *Encyclopedia of Phenomenology,* (Kluwer Academic Publishers, Dordrecht, 1997), p. 191.
26. Husserl, E. *Logical Investigations,* Translated by J.N. Findlay, (Routledge & Kegan Paul, London, 1970), Vol. 1, p. 339-40, (our emphases).
27. Ibid., p. 339.
28. Ibid., p. 337.

2

Moore's Intuitionism and the Phenomenological Value-Ethics

We propose now to delineate some of the important ideas of G.E. Moore, and see how they have close resemblance with that of phenomenological ethicists with regard to values. Our point of interest is to focus on the connectedness of Moore's thinking on goodness with the way some of the phenomenological value-theorists develop the matrix of phenomenological thinking with regard to values. Moore's thinking on goodness, in our view, seems to have a similarity on a few points with the phenomenological mode of understanding values, though each of the modes of thinking belongs to two different philosophical traditions. Moore, on the one hand, is said to have initiated the analytic tradition of philosophizing, and the phenomenological style of philosophizing begins with the writings of Husserl, on the other. That Moore and the phenomenological value-theorists share some points with regard to values has, indeed, been duly acknowledged by one of the most prominent value-theorists, namely, Max Scheler in his preface to the second edition of his book, *Formalism in Ethics and Non-Formal Ethics of Values.* He says,

> In England, G.E. Moore has set forth similar views (such as those developed by Scheler himself) on many points concerning the problem of values.[1]

In what follows, we shall bring out as clearly as possible these points of similarities that Moore's theory of good has with the phenomenological theories of value as formulated by both Scheler and Hartmann.

1. Moore and Scheler

1. In his preface to the *Principia Ethica*, Moore sets out his objective by raising two questions, namely, (a) "what kind of things ought to exist for their own sakes?" and (b) "what kind of actions ought we to perform?" He answers the first question by saying that it is the intrinsic goodness which ought to exist for its own sake. This statement, he readily acknowledges, is not susceptible of proof. For, the self-subsistent nature of goodness can only be non-sensibly intuited. The truth or falsity of intrinsic goodness lies in itself and nothing existing outside can make it true or false. No external evidence is of use to be adduced to prove it true or false.

But the answer to the second question is capable of proof or disproof. Moore's answer to this question is that one ought to do such action which would produce maximum intrinsic goodness. The evidence adduced in support of what one ought to do is of empirical kind and therefore, is of causal sort. And this question can be answered, according to Moore, by performing an empirical inspection.

Our point of interest in the present context is that the answer to the second question is dependent on the answer to the first question. That is, one has to *first* intuit what goodness is in its own sake, and then only can one decide what action ought to be performed. Here, the intuition of intrinsic goodness makes it possible for one to pass a judgement as to what he ought to do. There is involved a kind of *foundationalism*, in our view, in Moore when he asserts that intuition of goodness is the basis of moral decisions and judgements.

This sort of foundationalism, in the realm of value-ethics, seems to have been adopted by phenomenological ethicists as well. Scheler, for example, talks of intuition of values or what he calls "value-facts" which is the *basis* of philosophical ethics. For him, values are essences in phenomenological sense, or what he calls "phenomenological facts" as distinguished from natural and scientific facts. These value-facts are the objects of eidetic intuition having their specifiable contents. Now, in order to make value-judgements, it is necessary first to have cognition of values. It is non-sensible, direct and immediate intuition of values, according to Scheler, which paves the way for one to pass a value-judgement. All judgements concerning goods and acts of persons must "conform" to these value-facts in order to be *a priori* true. As Scheler states,

> All judgments must conform to *facts,* and "methods" are *purposeful* only insofar as they lead to propositions conforming to facts.[2]

In context of ethics, the statement would mean that all value-judgements would make sense only when they are "fulfilled" in value-facts. In other words, value-judgements can only be true when they are "clarified" in the light of the value-contents or when they receive their determination from such contents. Here, it is in this sense that value-intuitions are the *foundations* of value-judgements. In fact, philosophical ethics is possible only when the fact of non-sensible intuition of values is presupposed. For, the latter is at the root of the former.

2. Moore's idea of "naturalistic fallacy", in our view, has a close resemblance with Husserl's critique of naturalism. For Moore, naturalism is "a particular method of approaching Ethics … . This method consists in substituting for 'good' some one property of a natural object or of a collection of natural objects."[3] There are some ethical theories, according to Moore, which are built upon naturalism and they commit what he calls the "naturalistic fallacy" by identifying goodness with any one natural property.

In order to understand his criticism against naturalism in ethics, we should keep in mind Moore's general standpoint that "good is a property of certain natural objects", but "good itself is not a natural property". For Moore, good is not to be assimilated with the natural properties, such as, pleasure, tall, red, etc. The nature of natural predicates is such that they are descriptive in character, and that they describe the natural objects. They are not used to judge any natural object or action whether they are valuable or not. They cannot give us direction to our actions and hence to our life. But, on the contrary, moral predicates, such as, 'good', 'right', etc. are such that they evaluate our actions or prescribe what one ought to do as also evaluate natural objects.

They provide us with the guidelines for doing this or that action as principles. The *natural* terms and the *value*-terms should not be confounded with each other. The standpoint that maintains the non-identity of value and the natural properties has come to be known as ethical non-naturalism.

Moore's non-naturalistic standpoint drives him to undertake a critique of naturalism in ethics. He explicates what he calls "naturalistic fallacy" thus,

> It may be true that all things which are good are *also* something else, just as it is true that all things which are yellow produce a certain kind of vibration in the light. And it is a fact, that Ethics aims at discovering what are those other properties belonging to all things which are good. But far too many philosophers have thought that when they named those other properties they are actually defining good; that these properties, in fact, were simply not 'others,' but absolutely and entirely the same with goodness. This view I propose to call the 'naturalistic fallacy' ...[4]

What is suggested in the passage is that the fallacy essentially consists in identifying or equating any two notions which, in fact, are distinct or of supposing two words to be synonymous which they are not. For example, if one defines pleasure (i.e., identifies it with) as the sensation of blue, he would be committing the naturalistic fallacy. If the value "good" and the natural properties are not distinguished apart, according to Moore, a factual science will replace Ethics. That is, defining "good" in terms of natural properties would cause the occurrence of a factual science. This criticism against naturalism in ethics has been found to have resemblance with German idealists. A student of Husserl, Marvin Farber writes in the following way:

> With no apparent conscious motivation, a writer like G.E. Moore appears to point to an impasse to naturalism in ethics, and to be trying to achieve what idealists in Germany had wanted to accomplish in more elaborate ways.[5]

Thus it is clear that even though Moore, who obviously belongs to the British tradition of analytic or linguistic philosophy, definitely favours a critique of naturalism that brings him closer to the tradition of continental philosophers on this issue.

The above statement by Farber provides us a cue to enquire into the German philosophers' approaches that are against naturalism in ethics. At the outset, we find that Husserl abhors naturalism while formulating his theoretical as well as practical philosophy. It is the absurdities of naturalism in the theoretical sphere which has led Husserl to reject practical philosophy based on naturalism. According to Husserl, naturalism is a pre-philosophical attitude towards a commonly experienced world, which attempts to synthesize a "scientific" philosophy out of the results of the positive sciences. Husserl says,

> Characteristic of all forms of extreme and consistent naturalism is on the one hand the naturalizing of consciousness, including all intentionally immanent data of consciousness, and on the other the naturalising of ideas and consequently of all absolute ideals and norms.[6]

He believes that

> ... philosophy's role is to provide a foundation for normative discipline (ethics, axiology, etc.) – the ideal disciplines that transcend facts – he shows that no science of facts can provide them with a foundation. Because modern psychology is essentially bound up to the physical, it shares the naivete of all natural sciences; it is caught up in the contingency of empirical existence and cannot itself be absolute or necessary.[7]

The naturalist's attempt to "naturalise" the data of consciousness and of absolute norms and ideals, according to Husserl, is detrimental to the normative disciplines like ethics, aesthetics, etc. For, this sort of approach disregards the essences with which consciousness is constantly in touch. It is for this reason that Husserl rejects all ethics based on inductive experience. As Shmueli says on behalf of Husserl,

> *Against naturalistic theories* Husserl stresses the difference of values from physical or psychological qualities. They have their own general essence, and their validity does not depend on their actualisation in reality which is the domain of the time and space dimensions.[8]

It is no wonder that Scheler, who develops his value-ethics on Husserlian methodology, would reject naturalism in ethics. He carefully distinguishes values from the natural objects which are their bearers. For Scheler, the being of values is independent of things, state-of-affairs, men and relations of all kinds, the so-called goods. For example, one considers a poem or a work of art as "beautiful" or "ugly" without knowing in the least which properties of work prompt the judgment. As Scheler writes,

> A value precedes its object; it is the first "messenger" of its particular nature. An object may be vague and unclear while its value is already distinct and clear.[9]

Further, that values are different from their bearers, Scheler argues, is clear from the fact that values themselves do not change with the changes that occur in their bearers. For example, value of friendship remains unchanged even if a friend of mine turns out to be a false friend and betrays me. Furthermore, values are also different from what people values or considers important. For example, a painting by Bikash Bhattacharjee is beautiful, not because what people think of it according to social validity, but because it is claimed that the beauty is found *in* the painting independently of people's opinion. Values are objective "facts". What Scheler seeks to clarify is the idea that values are a unique object, and like Moore, he establishes that values are not to be confounded with anything else – natural or metaphysical.

3. In the *Principia Ethica,* Moore's primary question is: What is 'good'? Or, how good is to be defined? Here he is concerned not with the definition of the word 'good' but with that "object or idea" which the "word is generally used to stand for."[10] This very "object or idea", for Moore, is good the nature of which he intends to discover. For him, "good" denotes a property or a quality which is of non-natural kind.

This view has a closer affinity with the phenomenological value-theorists according to whom values are non-natural essences. In the *Ideas I,* Husserl uses Plato's "*eidos*" synonymously with "essence" without committing himself to Plato's ontology of essences. Like Moore, Scheler too asserts values to be "objects". In his own words, "As value-phenomena ... values are *true objects* ... ."[11] Elsewhere, he calls values "genuinely objective objects."[12]

Having ascribing to values the status of "objects", both Moore and Scheler alike deny the conceptual status and consequently the definability of values. To understand the point, let us first take up Moore's view. Moore says,

> If I am asked 'what is good?' my answer is that good is good, and that is the end of the matter. Or if I am asked 'How is good to be defined?' my answer is that it cannot be defined, and that is all I have say about it.[13]

This sense of 'definition' in which Moore is denying the definability of goodness is definition by analysis. This kind of definition "states what are the parts which invariably compose a certain whole."[14] That is, to define in this sense means to analyse, or to break up a complex into its simplest constituent parts, which cannot be further analysed or broken. Goodness refers to a simple property having no parts. Its simplicity lies in its very nature of substantial and indivisible character. Moore's claim is that goodness is indefinable means that it can*not* be analysed in any conceptual terms, as for him, goodness is not a concept, but an "object or idea", and what it denotes is a property or a quality. The term 'definition' in general means, a statement of precise meaning of a concept and this is always given in term of language. Moore's view finally is that the definition of goodness which is an "object or idea" is impossible anyhow, and any effort to define it is bound to be a failure. The point is significant for Scheler, as for him too values are not concepts but ideal *essences*. Scheler asks us to distinguish essences from concepts while elaborating his phenomenological method. He writes,

> The concept "thing" and the intuited "thingness", the concept equality and the equality, or the being-equal (as distinguished from the being similar), etc., must be clearly distinguished.[15]

Elsewhere, he unambiguously states that

> ... values are not concepts abstracted from empirical, concrete things, men, or deeds; nor are they abstract, "dependent" moments of such things. They are *independent phenomena* that are comprehended independent of the peculiarity of contents,

> as well as of the being-real or the being-ideal and the non-being (in this two-fold sense) of their bearers.[16]

We have already stated above that Scheler refers values to be "objects" and by that he means, according to Moosa, two things: (i) "They (values) are not mere concepts but are actually given in intuition,"[17] and (ii) "they are not merely abstracted from things, deeds or persons."[18] This means, for Scheler, that values are *independent phenomena* having "autonomous being"[19] of their own. And values being "phenomena" are not amenable to definition as the latter is always rendered in conceptual terms. "Definition of the phenomena, according to Scheler essentially impossible anyhow … ."[20] In Scheler's words, "The concept of value does not allow any more of a definition than the concept of being does."[21] Thus for both Moore and Scheler, values being "object" or "phenomena" cannot be defined.

4. Now our question is: how are values known? In order to answer the question, it seems that both Moore and Scheler share, at least initially, an identical model of moral epistemology. According to Moore, good is known by intuition. He says that whenever a person

> thinks of 'intrinsic value', or 'intrinsic worth', or says that a thing 'ought to exist,' he has before his mind the unique object – the unique property of things – which I mean by 'good.'[22]

This means that when we judge anything to be good, we have before our mind's eye, a unique object called good. And this is what is meant by intuition of goodness for Moore. Though Moore does not have further analysed the nature of the kind of intuition which, according to him, responsible for having the cognition of goodness, but the context in which he talks of it, he seems to "consider it to be a non-sensuous mode of direct awareness."[23] This sort of intuition is *direct* in the sense that it operates without recourse to any mediated means, such as, concepts, symbols signs, or instruction.

The kind of intuition which has been elaborated above seems, in our view, to be closely akin to what has been called by Scheler variously as "essential intuiting" or "phenomenological intuition."[24] The phenomenological intuition is also a kind of *immediate* and *direct* apprehension quite as Moore seems to think of intuition. This is amply clear in what Scheler states,

> Phenomenological experience alone yields facts "themselves" and, hence, immediately, i.e., not in a way mediated by symbols, signs, or instructions of any kind.[25]

5. Finally, it may be interesting to note that both Moore and Scheler find values quite comparable with colour. Let us see in the following passage how Moore compares goodness with yellowness. Moore says,

> My point is that 'good' is a simple notion, just as 'yellow' is a simple notion; that, just as you cannot, by any manner of means, explain to any one who does not already know it, what yellow is, so you cannot explain what good is.[26]

The comparison of goodness with yellowness made by Moore is not to show that they have some objective characteristics in common, because they have no such objective characteristics. Moore's intention of making this comparison is to clarify that goodness is simple, indefinable and immediately apprehensible as implied in the above passage. In A.C. Ewing's words,

> Goodness is of course a very different kind of characteristic from a colour, but they might still well resemble each other in being immediately apprehended and in being indefinable.[27]

Turning to Scheler, we see that he too refers to the analogy that values share with colours. But it seems to us that he goes beyond Moore in comparing values with colour and seeks to focus on a much wider issue relating to values. We have already seen that there is concurrence between Scheler and Moore on the point of values being indefinable and directly and immediately intuitable. But Scheler seems to have gone beyond Moore to show (i) that values "exist" in the way a pure colour of the spectrum exists, and (ii) that "value-qualities, however, are *'ideal objects,'* as are qualities of colors and sounds."[28]

In concluding, we may observe that though Scheler's *Formalism in Ethics* does not open with the analysis of the nature of good as we find in Moore's *Principia Ethica,* he does not take good as the highest moral value as Moore does but only as something which is attached to the act that realizes a positive value.

2. Moore and Hartmann

It may be relevant here to put Hartmann's value-Platonism in the context of Moore's theory of goodness in order to have a better understanding of the former. This has been done by Professor Cadwallader[29] by bringing out the points of contrast and convergence between Moore and Hartmann in the following way.

We may begin by elaborating a fundamental point of contrast between Moore and Hartmann. Both of them may be said to have advocated Platonism in their respective theories of values, though in different senses. In her talk about what a value is in the context of value-Platonism, Cadwallader has made a distinction between a *thing, event* or *conduct* and the *standard* or *norm* by reference to which it is judged to be valuable, that is, between *what* is valued, and that by *which* it is valued. The former is termed as "actualized value" and the latter as "value-ideal".

Keeping in mind this important distinction, let us see whether Moore's goodness is an actualized value or is it a value-ideal, and bring out a contrast between these two thinkers. The actualized values are things or events of our value-experience and a part of the sensible world. Obviously, they are *in time*. They are something concrete and judged to be valuable by some subject. The relationship to a subject is a necessary condition for the existence of actualized values. They are not properties – natural or non-natural. But goodness is a property and not a thing or event of the actualized world. Therefore, Moore's goodness is not an actualized value.

Now, Moore's goodness is not a value-ideal in the Platonic sense either. For Moore, goodness, in the first place, is a *property*, though non-natural in kind. It is a property *of* and *in* the natural world. As Moore writes,

> ... I do not deny that good is a property of certain natural objects: certain of them, I think, *are* good; and yet I have said that 'good' itself is not a natural property.[30]

To say that goodness is a non-natural property does not by implication mean that it is a value-ideal in the Platonic sense. For value-ideals, by contrast, are not properties, and they belong to an "ideal realm", which is beyond the sensible world of space and time. Therefore, Moore's goodness is *not* a Platonic value-ideal. It is, according to Cadwallader, a third kind of thing. Thus in pursuance of these arguments, she concludes that Moore's theory of good cannot be said to be Platonism properly so called but merely a *property*-Platonism.

Hartmann's value-theory, on the other hand, is a value-Platonism-proper inasmuch as in his theory, values are avowedly given a status of Platonic Ideas. Values, according to Hartmann, have ideal, and not actual, self-existence. They are neither actualized values nor are they properties of natural objects. They belong not to the actual world but to an *ideal* world of Platonic type. They are, therefore, value-ideal.

Let us now turn to some points of convergence between the views of Moore and Hartmann with regard to values. *First,* values have been conceived of by both Moore and Hartmann as *ontologically unique* in their mode of existence. Values share some aspects of their existence with some other objects. For Moore, goodness is a simple quality like *yellow* on the one hand, and for Hartmann, values are like *logico-mathematical* objects, on the other. And, for both of them, values are different from their analogues.

Secondly, according to both Moore and Hartmann, values are *non*-natural objects. For the former, value (goodness) exists *in* this world as non-natural property of natural objects, but for the latter, values exist in a *different* realm of their own other than mundane reality. Again, for Moore, as a non-natural *property* of natural objects, it is in the world and yet, like natural objects, not in time.[31] For Hartmann, values being residents of the realm of Platonic Ideas are also not in time.

Thirdly, although for Moore, goodness is *not* in time, from this it does *not* follow that goodness is an *ideal* object. Because, for Moore, goodness is a *property* of natural object after all, though *itself non-natural.* Being a property and then a property of natural objects, goodness, Cadwallader argues, can*not* be regarded as an *ideal* object. For, what is ideal in Platonic sense can never belong to the natural world. And this is the reason for Moore to be called not value-Platonist-*proper,* but only a value-*property*-Platonist.

Fourthly, a value is an independently real entity for both Moore and Hartmann, in the sense that according to the former, value-properties, like all other properties, are "objective", and according to the latter, a value is a real existent apart from being known or appreciated. Moore claims objectivity of goodness by showing its analogy with perceptual qualities, such as, yellow; and Hartmann argues for objective validity of values by the analogy that values share with logico-mathematical objects. So, both of them seem to share *value-objectivism.* Thus Cadwallader concludes,

> Each in his own way insists that 'goodness' refers to something objective, that this "real thing" is not "merely subjective" despite the fact that actual cases (instances) of goodness always (or, according to Moore, usually) involve an experiencing subject.[32]

And *lastly,* a focal point of similarity between the axiological theories of Moore and Hartmann is that, according to both these theories, good is "indefinable". However, both of them adduce different reasons for a similar standpoint. For Moore, "... good has no definition because it is simple and has no parts."[33] On the other hand, Hartmann writes, "good is not definable – neither directly, *per genus et differentiam* nor indirectly",[34] and the reasons are that (1) "... values are many, their realm is a manifoldness; and (2) we know neither the entire manifoldness nor its unity."[35] Hartmann argues for the indefinability of goodness not because it is too *simple* but because it is too complex.

Besides the points above as brought out by Professor Cadwallader, we may add the following points in the context of Moore-Hartmann relationship with regard to values: (i) In our view, Hartmann also shares the sort of foundationalism as advocated by both Moore and Scheler that we mentioned earlier. He distinguishes between two kinds of apprehension: one which he calls "primary consciousness of value", and the other is "secondary". In its "secondary" sense, that is, the judgemental nature of moral values is based on the "primary" sensing of values. In other words, moral judgement is grounded on the "phenomenological intuition" of values. It is on this primary "sensing" of values, according to Hartmann, that the whole of philosophical ethics is founded. That is, the latter presupposes the former for its foundation. As Hartmann writes,

> In any case one may in a certain sense say that philosophical ethics discovers values. But very seldom is it a really *original* discovery. Generally it is a later appropriation of that which beforehand existed in the moral consciousness, and which was active there, whether as an accepted commandment of current morality or as an unconscious point of view in the sensing of values within their real setting.[36]

What Hartmann calls "sensing of values" in the above sense, is the original discovery and is the basis of all philosophical ethics, the latter being judgemental in nature. The discovery of values by philosophical ethics is what he calls "discovery at second hand". Thus Moore and Hartmann alike are concerned with the placing of value-intuition as lived processes of "experience" at the origin of their respective philosophical ethics, though they belong to two distinctly different philosophical traditions. *This* concern, what we call *ethical foundationalism,* is endorsed by both Moore and Hartmann.

(ii) Further, if we look at Hartmann's theory of value-experience, it would be clear that he would support Moore on the point that values are not concepts but *essences* in Platonic form, and thus they cannot be defined in conceptual terms. *This* is implied in the following passage:

> If an age has impressed a name upon a perceived value, it is the very next generation which is certain not to give any longer the same meaning to the name. Words are sluggish, concepts are coarse and come hobbling after, but *insight* into values is inconceivably alert and highly differentiated; thought cannot tell what it will do next.[37]

(iii) Hartmann avowedly accepts the theory of intuition as it is given by Scheler. He has termed this sort of intuition as "primary consciousness of value". Like Moore, Hartmann too stresses the immediate capacity of intuition to apprehend the values. He clarifies,

> Every moral preference is intuitive, is immediately there and is always contained in the grasping of a given circumstance (whether it be a situation or a finished course of conduct). It does not first wait for a judgement of the understanding.[38]

Here our point is *not* that Moore's concept of intuition absolutely identical with that of Scheler or Hartmann's. Rather, what is meant by intuition on Moore's view comes closer to that of the phenomenologists, in the sense that, for both, intuition is a *non-sensuous, direct* and *immediate* kind of cognition which may be conceived of as pre-linguistic or pre-conceptual means of cognition.

Let us now summarize the points, in conclusion. We have endeavoured to show that Moore, on the one hand, and the phenomenological thinkers like Husserl, chiefly Scheler and Hartmann, on the other, despite their affiliations to two *different* philosophical traditions, develop similar views on some points with regard to values. *First,* there is a sort of *foundationalism* both in Moore's theory of good as well as in the phenomenological theories of value. *Secondly,* both Moore and Husserl make an appeal to their reader to get over of the context of *naturalism* in ethics. Scheler is also with them on the point that values are a unique kind of objects which are quite different from their bearers. *Thirdly,* for Moore as also for Scheler and Hartmann, values are not mere concepts but are "*objects*", and therefore, they are *indefinable. Fourthly,* both Moore and the phenomenological thinkers found values to be directly and immediately intuitable. *Fifthly,* both Moore and Scheler compare values with colours to render clear the points perspicuous. And in the second section, it was shown that though Hartmann takes on value-Platonism in a different sense as advocated by Moore, yet he shares with Moore some points with regard to values.

Notes

1. Scheler, M. *Formalism in Ethics and Non-Formal Ethics of Values,* (Henceforth, *Formalism in Ethics*). Translated by Manfred S. Frings and Roger L. Funk, (Northwestern University Press, Evanston, 1973), p. xxi.

2. Ibid., p. 52.
3. Moore, G.E. *Principia Ethica,* (Cambridge University Press, London, 1965), p. 40. It is to be noted here that in this chapter, "good" and "goodness" have been used interchangeably to purportedly refer to the same property as Moore does. Though Moore uses "good" in most places, he also uses "goodness" as well. For example, please see, p. 10 of the *Principia Ethica.*
4. Ibid., p. 10.
5. Farber, M. *Phenomenology and Existence,* (Harper & Row Publishers, New York, 1967), p. 166.
6. Husserl, E. *Phenomenology and the Crisis of Philosophy,* Translated with notes and introduction by Quentin Lauer, (Harper & Row Publishers, New York, 1965), p. 80.
7. Please see Quentin Lauer's Introduction to Husserl's *Phenomenology and the Crisis of Philosophy,* op. cit. pp. 9-10.
8. Shmueli, E. "The Universal Message of Husserl's Ethics: An Explication of Some Ethical Premises in Transcendental Phenomenology", in Tymieniecka (ed.), *Analecta Husserliana,* Vol. XXII, p. 554.
9. Scheler, M. *Formalism in Ethics,* op. cit. p. 18.
10. Moore, G.E. *Principia Ethica,* op. cit. p. 6.
11. Scheler, M. *Formalism in Ethics,* op. cit. p. 19.
12. Ibid., p. 255.
13. Moore, G.E. *Principia Ethica,* op. cit. p. 6.
14. Ibid., p. 9.
15. Scheler, M. *Formalism in Ethics,* op. cit. p. 49.
16. Ibid., p. 185.
17. Moosa, I. "A critical examination of Scheler's justification of the existence of values", *The Journal of Value Inquiry,* Vol. 25, 1991.
18. Ibid.
19. Scheler, M. *Formalism in Ethics,* op. cit. pp. 186-87.
20. Spiegelberg, H. *The Phenomenological Movement,* (Martinus Nijhoff, The Hague, 1971), p. 243.
21. Frings, M.S. "The Background of Max Scheler's 1927 Reading of *Being and Time: A* Critique of a Critique Through Ethics", *Philosophy Today,* Vol. 36, No. 2/4, Summar, 1992. This passage is translated and quoted by Manfred Frings from Scheler's *Gesammelte Werke,* Bouvier Verlag, Bonn, 1985 published in the article referred to above.
22. Moore, G.E. *Principia Ethica,* op. cit. p. 17.
23. Prasad, R. "Moore on the Indefinability of Goodness", in *Karma, Causation and Retributive Morality,* (Indian Council of Philosophical

Research, New Delhi in association with Munshiram Manoharlal Publishers (P) Ltd., New Delhi,1989), p. 165.

24. Scheler, M. *Formalism in Ethics,* op. cit. p. 48.
25. Ibid., p. 50.
26. Moore, G.E. *Principia Ethica,* op. cit. p. 7.
27. Ewing, A.C. *Ethics,* (The English Universities Press Ltd., London, 1969), p. 88.
28. Scheler, M. *Formalism in Ethics,* op. cit. p. 21.
29. Please see E.H. Cadwallader's *Searchlight on Values*, Chapter II, (University Press of America, New York, 1984).
30. Moore, G.E. *Principia Ethica,* op. cit. p. 41.
31. Moore makes it a criterion for the natural objects that they "exist in time" (*Principia Ethica,* p. 40), and by implication, it follows that non-natural objects are *not* in time. Therefore, good as a non-natural property is not in time.
32. Cadwallader, E.H. *Searchlight on Values,* op. cit. p. 42.
33. Moore, G.E. *Principia Ethica,* op. cit. p. 9.
34. Hartmann, N. *Ethics.* Translated by Stanton Coit, (George Allen & Unwin Ltd., London, 1958), Third Impression, Vol. II, p. 172.
35. Ibid., p. 88.
36. Ibid., Vol. I, p. 87, (our emphasis).
37. Ibid., p. 88, (our emphasis).
38. Ibid., p. 176.

3

Hartmann's Critique of Kant's Ethical Framework

The depth and profundity of Kant's ethical thinking did not escape the notice of subsequent moral philosophers. Among others, in recent times, the phenomenological ethicists have sharply responded to Kant's ethical ideas, which have exercised a powerful and pervasive influence over the centuries down to the present era. Nicolai Hartmann is one such thinker who has duly recognized some aspects of importance in Kantian ethics, though he is highly critical of some other aspects of his ethical thinking. In point of fact, Hartmann has devoted a section of his *Ethics* for a critical appraisal of Kant's ethics. In this chapter, we propose to delineate, explicate, and reflect on Hartmann's criticism of Kant's ethical framework under three different sections, viz., (i) Subjectivism in Kant, (ii) Formalism in Kant, and (iii) Intellectualism in Kant.

1. Subjectivism in Kant

Hartmann has situated his own ethics in opposition to Kant's ethical framework. He finds himself in line with the historical perspective, that is, the perspective which regards values as concrete *a priori* essences, and Kant, according to him, is an exception to the entire historical perspective. As he writes,

> almost all philosophical ethics, although standing only half-way towards the solution of its problems, yet deserving the name of ethical research, has been fundamentally a concrete ethics of

> values. Kant, on the contrary, and his followers are the exception in the historical succession. They constitute a chasm which separates us from the great traditions of antiquity and of the Middle Ages.[1]

Elsewhere he says,

> For it was Kant who set up the unity of the moral law instead of the concrete variety of the virtues, the formal principle in place of the fulness of content, and subjective legislation in the position held by the objective essence of moral ideas. On account of this contrast, the present-day investigation of values finds very little solid ground under its feet.[2]

Let us now look at Hartmann's critique of Kant's "subjectivism" of practical reason. First, the concept of will, or what Kant calls "good will", is accorded primary importance in Kant's ethics. The will is that which initiates the action. The will does not mean mere wish to do something. It means taking a decision to act or perform according to a maxim. But the ground of its determination does not lie in itself. Nor does it have its locus in the nature of man or in the circumstances of the world in which an agent is placed, but in the pure practical reason. It is Reason in its practical use or function which determines the will. The practical reason exerts influence on the will by means of moral imperative. At this stage, Hartmann raises a question as to how one can understand the relation between value and the will.

In responding to the question, Hartmann says that the will has the power only to choose to either carry out or not the commandments. It cannot itself issue forth any commandments. Commandments or the moral law can be issued only by a source or agency other than or outside of the will. That agency is the independent realm of objective values themselves. In other words, the values themselves are the source of issuing commandments. These commandments are addressed to the will. That is, the commandments or the moral laws have the validity for the will only. Since the will has the power and freedom to choose whether to carry out the commandments, it retains its autonomy even though the commandments come from outside the will.

For Kant, the source of commandments is the will, which also acts as the agent for carrying out the commandments. Thus, the will has a double function: (a) of issuing commandments and (b) of carrying out or not carrying out the commandments. According to Hartmann, (a) is not necessary for the autonomy of the will, because the autonomy of the will consists in (b).

The consequence of above stated position of Kant is that it makes the Ought subservient to the will. The will is something subjective, that is, it resides in a moral subject and therefore, it cannot supply us with something objective. The will, as a subjective principle, cannot issue an objective principle. That is, the Ought, as an objective principle of morality, cannot originate from the will that belongs to a moral subject. The Ought, for having its authoritative character, cannot make itself subordinate to a subjective principle. The error of Kant, according to Hartmann, lies in placing the Ought under something which is not itself a value. In Kant's ethics, it is the will, instead of value, that has been given an authority to set up the moral standard. Thus the Ought, in Kant's ethical framework, originates from the subjective principle.

Hartmann's general observation on the Kantian doctrine of subjectivism is that the latter is the general direction of his philosophical enterprise. This is characterized by saying that whatever has the nature of principle originates from the subject. For example, Kant's concept of space and time are "a priori intuition" of the subject, the categories are "the pure concepts of understanding", and the unity of objective knowledge is given by "synthetic unity of apperception". In other words, in Kant's philosophy, the subject comes to rank higher and thus surpasses the object, and the object, in a way, remains subordinated to the subject. In other words, the latter always determines the former.

What follows is that Kant legitimizes the subject with authority to issue the commandments and thereby to set up the standard of what ought to be done. This has been summarized by Hartmann as follows:

> ... the will determines or creates the values, not the values the will. The will is, then, not bound to something which in itself has value, but value is nothing else than an expression for that towards which the will is directed. Values are directional concepts of the pure will.[3]

Secondly, the transcendental subjectivism of Kant poses some serious difficulties in understanding the problem of freedom of the will. The will, which is supposed to be the originator of the principles of morality, has the freedom to follow it or not. But the question is: how can the will transgress that principle which is laid down by itself?

Hartmann's point against Kant may be understood in the following way. Kant claims both autonomy *and* freedom for the will. If the will is really autonomous, then it claims to be so only on the ground that it is the originator of its own laws. If that be so, how can the will transgress that which it makes *intrinsically* for itself? For example, the nature cannot violate its own laws, even though it may well claim to be autonomous with regard to its role as originator of laws. On the other hand, if the will claims to be free on the ground that it has the freedom either to conform to its laws or to transgress them, then can it really claim to be the originator of laws? The point that Hartmann is trying to drive home is that Kant's view, that the will is both free and autonomous, involves a contradiction in terms. "For Kant", Hartmann avers,

> the pure will is accepted as free, exactly in so far as it has no other ground of determination than the principle which inheres in its own essence. Consequently Kant's "free" will has in truth, on the basis of these determinations, self-legislation (in the strict sense, "autonomy"), but has no freedom in the proper sense of the word. It is subject to the autonomous principle of its essence exactly as nature is subject to natural law.[4]

Thus, in Kant's ethics, it seems that the will can be free only by ceasing to be autonomous. Hartmann, therefore, concludes that "transcendental subjectivism is not only not required by the doctrine of the freedom of the will, but stands directly in opposition to it."[5]

Thirdly, Kant's subjective origin of the commandment cannot be justified if the freedom of the will is to be recognized. According to Kant, there can be two sources of the commandment or the moral law: one is the world of nature and the other is Reason. If it issues from the world of nature, then it would *not* be universal and autonomous as it would be merely a hypothetical imperative. And if it originates from Reason, then it would be universal, autonomous, *a priori*, and categorically imperative. Now, if we look at his characterization of the moral principle, then we shall see that, for Kant, the commandment or the moral principle must be *a priori* and categorical in character, and therefore, cannot be empirical and hypothetical in nature. From this, it follows that the commandment, according to Kant, must have its origin in Reason alone which, as we have seen, makes the Ought dependent upon the will.

In the language of modern logic, Kant's argument takes the form of a disjunctive inference in the *modus tollendo ponens* as it has been pointed out by Hartmann. That is, if we suppose that p for *the moral law emanates from nature,* and q for *it issues from reason*, then the syllogism would be of the form:

$$p \vee q$$
$$\sim p$$
$$\therefore q$$

The above syllogism would be valid if there exists no other possibilities other than the two mentioned above. But, according to Hartmann, there is a *third* possibility which has been excluded by Kant because of his basic assumption that whatever is aprioristic must be referred back to the pure and legislative practical reason. If the Kantian alternative would become "either a priori or a posteriori" instead of "either from nature or from reason", then there would no need of a third possibility. Since the denial of aposterioristic origin would lead to necessity of the aprioristic nature of the commandment. For Hartmann, however, *a priori* is identical with Platonic realm of values. But, for Kant, *a priori* is identical with Reason. Hartmann concludes,

> From it nothing can be disjunctively inferred. The exclusion of one member does not entail the setting up of the other. The concept of the aprioristic does not coincide with that of origin in reason. The alternative is false, the disjunction not complete. But with it the conclusion falls away. It is a false inference.[6]

It is quite understandable to Hartmann that Kantian subjectivism is not an ordinary one. For, unlike ordinary subjectivism, it is entirely based on *apriorism.* Kant's error is that he cannot but place the apriority in the subject itself because of his philosophical compulsion.

2. Formalism in Kant

Kant's theory of ethics has often been characterized by his critics as "formalism", and Hartmann too shares this point of criticism from his own point of view. According to Kant, the concept of duty and its formula, that is the Categorical Imperative, must be a formal law. That is, it is devoid of any "material" or content. It cannot give direction to *what* ought to be done. Kant argues that if the will receives its determination from the "material", that is, from the inclinations, desire or from the result it produces, then this kind of determination would be empirical and naturalistic, and that it cannot be rational. This sort of determination from naturalistic standpoint is heteronomous and cannot claim to be rational determination. For, according to Kant, what is rational is valuational. That is, a will must always seek its determination from the reason or rationality, and not in natural tendencies of a moral agent in the form of a commandment. In Hartmann's words,

> All "material" determination of the will is heteronomous, is derived from things and their relations which, on the ground of natural tendencies and impulses, appear to be worth striving for. A materially determined will is determined empirically – that is, "from outside." Material determination is naturalistic, not rational. It is not determination by the law and by the essence of the good. For the essence of the good is a purely formal quality of the will.[7]

This is what precisely constitutes Kant's formalism.

It has been noted by Hartmann himself that Kant's formalism has a background which can be traced back to ancient philosophy. The philosophy of Aristotle favours the pure form and neglects the matter. Matter is conceived of as something indeterminate, obscure and possessing a lower value. The form, on the other hand, is regarded as the determining principle; and it is the form which allows something to be valuable. The Aristotelian bias against matter is found also to be prevalent in the modern philosophy, particularly in the philosophy of Descartes and Leibnitz. It continues to play a major role in Kant's theory of knowledge as well as in his moral philosophy. The *Critique of Pure Reason* is entirely dominated by the contrast of matter and form. The matter or the "manifold" is supplied by the senses and the understanding applies a conceptual category to them and thus knowledge arises only from their union. In his *Critique of Practical Reason,* the similar trend is quite noticeable. The natural tendencies and inclinations are the "matter" and the Categorical Imperative is a law which is formal in character.

But one thing that merits attention at this point is that the categories, schemata, imperative and postulates, – all these principles, are formal and are at the same time *a priori*. Thus it follows that, for Kant, the *a priori* is identical with the formal. The *a priori* – *a posteriori* opposition has nothing to do with the duality of formal and material. Whatever is *a priori* is formal, and whatever is material is not aprioristic. It is true that whatever is *a priori* is universally valid but not the aposterioristic. But it is *not* true that universal character is always something formal. A principle, like moral commandment, can very well be material without throwing away its aprioristic character. Hartmann contends that a will determined by "matter" is not, as Kant thinks, empirically determined will. Because, the "matter" here does not mean natural tendencies such as pleasure or pain but something non-empirical, non-natural essences, that is, values which are aprioristic in nature. In Hartmann's words,

> Material determination is not naturalistic determination. It does not necessarily spring from general existential laws, it does not imply any causal dependency. It does not degrade the human will into a "natural entity." For its origin can be perfectly autonomous, its objectivity purely aprioristic.[8]

Hartmann readily acknowledges his agreement with Scheler on this point.

While criticizing Kant's formalism, Hartmann recognizes that there are some aspects of his ethics, which can be preserved without accepting its "formal" character. These are:

(i) Kant's rejection of empiricism and heteronomy in ethics and building up of a pure ethics which is cleansed of all empirical elements.

(ii) Kant's rejection of the view that moral principles can be derived from the goods by the will.

(iii) His claim of strict universal validity of the moral laws.

(iv) Kant's conviction that goodness belongs to the will itself and not to the end it pursues.

(V) Kant's rejection of casuistry.

3. Intellectualism in Kant

Though Kant has given sense-perception no less an important position in his philosophy, yet understanding or thought or Reason enjoys a superiority over the former. In his theoretical philosophy, the "givens" are primarily unsystematic and unordered sensations, which are received passively by our "understanding", and the latter gives them order and form, and thereby is constituted a concrete case of knowledge. Thus in the knowledge-process, understanding or thought has been given an active role to play – the role of law-giving to nature. Similarly, in his practical philosophy, it is Reason, in its practical use or function, which has been given the role of bestowing some meaning structure upon our chaotic states of inclinations and to issue moral commandments accordingly. Hence, in the dualism of sense and understanding, the nobility of the latter surpasses the former in Kant's philosophy. This is what has been dubbed by Hartmann as "intellectualism".

It would not have been a matter of concern for Hartmann, if it had not been for Kant to have identified this contrasted pair by implication with *a priori* and *a posteriori*. For Kant, sense-perception and sense-intuition are related to aposterioristic knowledge, whereas understanding, thought and Reason concern only aprioristic knowledge. However, his notion of "pure intuition" in the Transcendental Aesthetic and the doctrine of Schematicism of the categories are exceptions to the latter identification.

Hartmann then proceeds to repudiate the Kantian view that *a posteriori* is "sensible". According to Hartmann, what is "given" is not purely sensory content and contains a plenty of a priori elements, such as, the Kantian Categories. But Kant is not concerned with the objectivity of the natural objects but with "a gnoseological objectivity which is determined through the theoretical contrast to the aprioristic. The given, then, permits of being set up as equal to the evidence of the senses."[9] In this sense, the "given" is not something to be grasped as a phenomenon but something as a product of theory. So, the "given", i.e., the sensible is identified with the *a posteriori*.

This confusion of *a posteriori* with the sensible, according to Hartmann, has its adverse effect in ethics too. For Kant, an empirical ("material") determination of the will is always a determination of it by the senses, that is, by the pleasure and pain; and, this he calls the heteronomous determination. But, according to Hartmann, this is hardly the case. The will is never determined by the pleasure and pain but by the *objects.* We desire not for pleasure but the objects having a value accompanying it. It is, again, *not* the pleasure which makes certain things desirable but the *value* which goes with them. Pleasure and pain come only secondarily after the realization of a desire and are traced back by us as an effect of goods upon us. "What immediately hovers before the willing consciousness", Hartmann says,

> is always a task, the aim itself, and indeed something concrete and material … . The content of the thing willed transports the person willing beyond himself; it causes him to lose himself in the object, in his idea, in his identification with the thing willed.[10]

Hence, for Hartmann, "material" does not necessarily mean the sensible or the a posteriori.

Hartmann proceeds to his second point of criticism of Kant in this context which, according to him, is more important than the first point discussed above. He rejects the Kantian view that *a priori* coincides with the rational. Hartmann points out that though Kant does not *always* stick to this view as he speaks of *a priori intuition* of space and time in his Transcendental Aesthetic, yet rational/*a priori* has got a settled place in his philosophy. Categories are *a priori* "concepts of understanding" which bestows *form* of its own upon the "given" sensations and produces a judgement – a piece of knowledge. Kant's search for synthetic *a priori* rests upon the function of judgement. His objective of whole rational criticism concerns only the synthetic *a priori* judgement and *not a priori* knowledge in general. It is by means of a judgement, according to Kant, a thing or event can be grasped.

But in grasping a thing or an event, Hartmann points out, there is *no* trace of thinking or judging. In our knowledge of things or events, there obtains the *a priori* knowledge, which is intuitive in character and the judgement, in the form of which it is expressed, is something secondary and derivative. Thus Hartmann sums up:

> ... the natural comprehension of the world of things is from the beginning permeated with aprioristic elements; all comprehension is accomplished in categorical structures, and precisely herein consists the apriority of the latter. Kant understood this relation very exactly; in regard to it the expression "the condition of possible experience" is most instructive. Only the intellectualistic interpretation, the introduction of thought, of conception, of judgement, once again renders this great achievement ambiguous. In order to measure the extent of the transcendental conditionality, we must entirely disregard this interpretation.[11]

In his ethics too, Kant identifies the *ethical a priori* with the *rational a priori* and there also the latter takes the form of a judgement. As a result, Kant cannot but think of the moral law or the Categorical Imperative as issued *not* by the rational will or the practical reason. Kant's presupposition in this context is that the practical function of Reason penetrates into each moment of our moral life. It dominates the individual cases of our approval and disapproval of an action, our moral choice and resolution etc. in purely logical form. But Hartmann points out that Kant does not, however, take this "ethical logicism"[12] (as Hartmann calls it) to its extreme point. As for him, it is *not* the knowledge of the moral law but the "reverence for the moral law" that determines the will. Nevertheless, the logical scheme keeps dominating in Kant's ethics, which makes the actual significance of the *a priori* unintelligible.

Notes

1. Hartmann, N. *Ethics,* Translated by Stanton Coit, (George Allen & Unwin Ltd., London, 1967), Fourth Impression, Vol. I, p. 204.
2. Ibid.

3. Ibid., p. 158.
4. Ibid., p. 159.
5. Ibid., p. 160.
6. Ibid., p. 162.
7. Ibid., p. 166.
8. Ibid., p. 170.
9. Ibid., p. 172.
10. Ibid., pp. 173-74.
11. Ibid., p. 175.
12. Ibid., p. 176.

4

Kant's Ethical Framework: Scheler's Phenomenological Critique

Max Scheler's philosophy exhibits a distinct preoccupation with Kant's ethical views. From Scheler's writings, it appears that he recognizes the profundity and inherent greatness of Kant's ideas and cannot but have a dialogue with him, though he takes the task to be only as a "secondary objective" – the primary one being the establishment of his own views. At the beginning of his philosophical venture, Scheler finds Kantian formal ethics as "obstacle" to erect his own edifice of "material" ethics. And in order to pave the way for the latter, he undertakes a thorough examination of Kant's formal apriorism and some specific doctrines of the *Critique of Practical Reason*. It may be noted here that Scheler's critique of Kant is based on his general understanding of Kant's ethics, leaving aside the intricacies of the interpretation of Kantian texts. The kind of criticism Scheler intends to put forward against Kant is not "internal criticism". Rather, it is to provide an alternative standpoint, which is based on his phenomenological perspective. It is the latter, which provides him with the method and direction for such a critique. Our objective presently is to present the main issue of contention involved in Scheler's critique of Kant which we propose to work out under three different sections: (i) Critique of the Kantian Formalism, (ii) Critique of the Kantian *A priori*, and (iii) Critique of the Kantian Intellectualism.

1. Critique of the Kantian Formalism

Kant's theory of ethics has often been characterized by such of his critics as Hegel and others as "formalism". Since for him, an action will have moral worth only if it is done for the sake of duty and not from inclinations, desires, etc. or from consideration of what result it produces. The concept of duty and its formula (i.e., the Categorical Imperative) is a formal principle and not a material principle of action that depends on empirical aims and desires. This means that it cannot prescribe any "material" or content, that is, what one ought to do in a certain concrete situation. This is what, in precise, constitutes the Kantian "formalism".

Scheler definitely endorses this criticism from his own point of view, that is, from phenomenological standpoint. Scheler sets forth his ethics against the backdrop of Kantian formal ethics as it becomes evident from the very title of his work, *Formalism in Ethics and Non-formal Ethics of Values*. The term "non-formal" is identical with the term "material" that "pertains not to matter but to content, and is a technical term."[1] It is used by Scheler to mean value-content and is an antonym of formal. In Kant's philosophy, "material" means the unordered sensations which are given to empirical intuition. However, in the context of phenomenological experience and of which Scheler speaks, "material" refers to the data of *consciousness* and not the data of *sensation*. This data of consciousness may be variously called "phenomena" or "essences", and the mode in which they are grasped is *essential* intuition as opposed to *empirical* intuition in which unordered sensations are given. This new meaning of "material" in the context of Scheler's value-ethics is identical with what he calls "value-facts" and is an object of phenomenological intuition.

In the opening paragraph of his *Formalism in Ethics*, Scheler agrees to concede Kant's demand that morality must be grounded on unconditional *a priori* principles. The ethics based on "goods" and "purposes" cannot provide such an unconditional and legitimate basis for morality. The Kantian doctrine that has been kept intact in Scheler's ethics is Kant's rejection of any ethics that rests on anticipated realization of contingent goods and purposes. Scheler writes,

> Kant maintains that whenever we make the goodness or the moral depravity of a person, an act of will, a deed, etc., dependent on their relation to a realm of existing goods (or evils) posited as real, we make the goodness or depravity of the

> will dependent on the particular contingent existence of this realm of goods, as well as on its experiential knowability .... Any alteration in this realm of goods would be accompanied by a change in the sense and meaning of good and evil. Since such a realm of goods is continuously changing and moving throughout history, the moral value of the human will and being would also have to take part in the destiny of this realm.[2]

Thus, the entire domain of ethics would be reduced to an empirical, inductive and *a posteriori* discipline that involves relativism and historicist situationism. This type of ethics, according to Scheler, has rightly been rejected by Kant as "patent *nonsense*."[3] The same consideration, according to Scheler, is equally true with regard to the ethics based on "ends" or "purposes", which try to define good and evil in terms of ends and purposes, and reduces them to technical values subsisting under the servitude of ends or purposes in question. Scheler concurs with Kant in rejecting *any* ethics based on "ends" or "purposes," as it would be incapable of providing absolute standard for morality.

But Scheler differs from Kant as regards conclusion drawn by the latter from this insight. According to Scheler, Kant believes that he has demonstrated far *more* than he has. He supposes that he has shown that an ethics based on a solid foundation must exclude *any* material content of our will and desires as the presupposition of good and evil. *This*, in effect, excludes not only *goods* and *purposes* but also all non-formal *values*. In other words, Kant thinks that a well-founded ethics not only excludes goods and purposes but also the *values* in relation to which they are goods. In fact, Kant makes no attempt to distinguish anything like *non*-formal values from the goods or purposes. He simply keeps in abeyance the "object (material) of the faculty of desire" from the domain of ethics.[4] And finally, for Kant, neither the goods and purposes nor the "material" values can form the basis of a "metaphysic of morals". Thus leaving aside the "material" domain of will, Kant attempts to secure a rigorous foundation of ethics in *formalism* which, according to Scheler, is a false way of understanding morality. He, on the contrary, argues for a rigorous foundation of ethics on the basis of *material content* (i.e., values) *of the will*. Unlike Kant, Scheler distinguishes values from goods and gives the former the status of "independent phenomena" in the phenomenological sense. He identifies values with what he calls "material a priori" instead of Kant's "formal a priori" and elevates them to a level which Kant has reserved for the moral law.

Not only that. Scheler, unlike Kant, assigns to values an authoritative and autonomous character. Thus in Scheler's ethical scheme, values enjoy a privileged status as compared to that of Kant's moral law, but *this* is not at the cost of curtailing the role of moral imperatives in ethics. As Ronald Perrin rightly comments,

> By claiming for values an essential place within the realm of the will's moral activity, Scheler does not depreciate the worth of the moral law any more than the arrival of a new child in the family diminishes the worth of its previous and present members. On the contrary, the moral realm – like the domain of the family – is considerably enriched.[5]

According to Scheler, moral laws or imperatives originate from the grasping of values by human beings. In general, Scheler's view is that our primordial encounter with things and conduct is infused with the grasping of values and it is this *value-intuition* which is at the root of all our conceptualization. If this is the case, then the very possibility of Kant's Categorical Imperative should be at stake. For, the Categorical Imperative is judgmental, and therefore conceptual in character, and would also require having a foundation on value-intuition. But Kant provides no such foundation other than its *rational* status, and the rational in such a scheme stands for the formal.

Scheler rejects the Kantian view that there is only a formal lawfulness among moral or aesthetic values. Equally, he does not share Kant's concern to emphasize laws and imperatives as the fundamental "facts" of moral consciousness. Scheler criticizes Kant's deontological ethics as "blind", for it overlooks the primacy of value-phenomena. It fails to see that the moral imperative *already* presupposes the apprehension of values. He does not see the range of "facts" on the basis of which *a priori* ethics can be founded. Scheler says,

> ... he [Kant] asserts that the moral law is a "fact of pure reason" which is to be exhibited without recourse to another principle.

> Much as the last assertion points in the right direction, Kant fails to show us how such "facts," on which any a priori ethics must be based lest it remain an empty construction, are to be distinguished from facts of observation and induction, and how their establishment is to be distinguished from that of those which are rightly rejected as a basis. What is the difference between a "fact of pure reason" and a merely psychological fact? How can a "law," such as a "moral law," be called a "fact" (and a "law" is, as we know, a moral foundation according to Kant)?[6]

The point that needs to be stressed here is the distinction between *values* as facts and the *moral laws*, as facts of morality. The latter is something, which is made or fabricated by human reason. Here, a person endowed with reason acts as the legislator. But value-facts are constructed or fabricated by none. It is, according to Scheler, on this original basis, not on something made by human reason, our moral life is founded. Scheler therefore rejects the Kantian approach in this context as possessed of "purely constructivistic character".

2. Critique of the Kantian *A priori*

The notion of *a priori* occupies a central place in the philosophy of both Kant and Scheler. On the one hand, though Kant has not developed this notion as a separate philosophical theme in his writings, it works as one of the fundamental concepts in the formulation of his transcendental system. It is central to his "Copernican revolution" and constitutes his famous problem: "how are synthetic *a priori* judgments possible?" He also finds an unconditional foundation for his ethics on the *a priori* plane that is "cleansed of everything empirical". In his concern to secure a legitimate ground for scientific knowledge and moral conviction, he finds in it the possibility of *a priori* knowledge.

On the other hand, in Scheler's ethics, the notion of *a priori* lies at the heart of his "material" ethics as well as his critique of the Kantian formalism. He takes the *a priori* to mean:

> ... all those ideal units of meaning and those propositions that are self-given by way of an *immediate intuitive* content in the

> absence of any kind of positing (*Setzung*) of subjects that think them and of the real nature of those subjects, and in the absence of any kind of positing of objects to which such units of meaning are applicable.[7]

Like Husserl, Scheler identifies the *a priori* with the *content* of essential intuition. It is "phenomena" in phenomenological sense, which has nothing to do with the Kantian disjunction of "phenomena" and "noumena". It is "self-given," that is, given in one *intentional* act, and not produced by the faculty of understanding like the Kantian *a priori*. In ethical sphere, Scheler identifies it with values. It is this conception of *a priori* as "material" or content that constitutes Scheler's "material" ethics of values as against Kantian formal ethics. Let us now turn to Scheler's specific points of criticism against Kantian notion of the *a priori*.

1. Scheler right away declares that "the identification of the 'a priori' with the 'formal' is a *fundamental error* of Kant's doctrine."[8] His point is that the opposition "a priori – a posteriori" is in no sense equivalent to the opposition "formal-material," as Kant assumes. When, in fact, the former distinction is *absolute* one, the second one is *relative,* related only to the universality of concepts and propositions. Let us illustrate the point by taking Scheler's own example. The apriority of the logical propositions that "'A is B' and 'A is not B' cannot both be true at the same time" is *formal,* universally true for *any* object A and B. However, it is *material* in the sense that it is based on the essential insight into the *fact* that the being and non-being of something are irreconcilable in *essential* intuition. Similarly, it is possible to distinguish *logical form* from the *material content* in a proposition that is *a posteriori* valid. For such a proposition consists of subject, predicate and a copula and it also contains a *what,* that is, its "material" content. Now, the facts of observation by which it is verified are also the facts by which its logical form is fulfilled in essential intuition. Hence, Scheler shows the distinction between the "formal" and "material" both *within* the spheres of *a priori* and *a posteriori.* On Scheler's view, the contrasted pairs "formal-material" and "a priori-a posteriori", though intersecting, are not equivalent with each other.

2. Closely connected with this error, according to Scheler, is the identification of the material with the "sensible content" and the *a priori* with the formal elements or "thought," or what is added to "sensible content" by reason. This is an error, Scheler points out, which is taken over by Kant from Hume's atomistic empiricism. The "sensible content" designates not *what* actually determines a given content, say, a sound or a colour, but only the *way* it is given to us. For the "sensible" is not something that is *in* a sound or *in* a colour.

For Kant, as for the empiricist, the question is, "what can be given?" instead of "what is given?" implying thereby that nothing beyond sensory functions "can" be given at all to our experience. For Kant, the conclusion is inevitable that all contents of experience, for which sensory functions are lacking, (such as relation, forms, values, space, time, causality and the like) are *added* to it by the "forming activity" of the rational subject. As Scheler points out,

> The mistake is that one does not simply ask *what* is given in meaning (*meinenden*) intentionality *itself,* but instead one *mixes* into the question *extra*intentional viewpoints and theories (which may be only natural theories of everyday life) of an objective or even a causal sort. But in this simple question of *what* is given (in an act), one must focus solely on this *what.*[9]

Scheler's point is that leaving aside all extra-intentional conditions, one must "see" the given in phenomenological intuition which, unlike Kant's, is non-formal yet *a priori.* Therefore, on Scheler's view, the non-formal is not necessarily sensible as Kant thought, but something given to non-sensible intuition.

In order to make this point more clear, we may for a while turn to Hume's empiricism. Hume's atomistic empiricism involves taking note of impressions as they occur in unending series of particulars. As he rightly points out, on purely empirical grounds there is no direct evidence of any relation between these particular impressions; hence there is no particular impression of, say, causal relation between any of these impressions. Hume is right that causality cannot be proved by rational demonstration or by direct perception. On this ground, Hume claims that there is no *necessity* (or necessary connection between impressions) in nature. It is only by habit or custom, as Hume puts it, that we relate any two impressions as cause and effect after successive occurrences in a uniform pattern.

Significantly, it is this atomistic empiricism that provokes Kant into saying that he had been aroused by "dogmatic slumber". Kant quite sees Hume's point but goes on to argue that necessity is imposed on nature by the mind. Kant's transcendental idealism carries the message that even though all knowledge begins with experience it does not end with it. His scheme of the categories of understanding provides for the way the world is experienced under conditions imposed by the knowing mind. The point of it is that anything that is given as sensible manifold would be subject to knowing mind's conditions of knowledge (in terms of categories of understanding).

It is this to which Scheler responds by pointing out underlying subjectivism in Kantian enterprise of knowledge. This leads him to look for that domain of non-sensible content, which would not be subject to any conditions imposed by the knowing mind. Grasping of essences, for Scheler, would involve coming to grips with this "material" by means of non-sensible intuition. In another context, while discussing Husserl's critical response to Kant, R.A. Mall has this to say:

> The necessity that we have in judgments while judging about something is of a different type than the necessity we feel in respect of the judged things. The former is a necessity of human thought in general, whereas the latter is a felt necessity of the objective type. In the former, we have just a fact of the psychology of human thinking. The latter is a part and parcel of our insight of its not being able to be otherwise. Hume was nearer the truth when he maintained that there are different types of necessities. If the differentia of necessity is its force and certainty, Hume was right in pointing at the necessity embedded in belief.[10]

Precisely it is this point Scheler too takes up against Kant, namely, that of subjectivising knowledge by imposing the conditions of knowing mind.

The Kantian question "what can be given?" means under what *conditions* anything can be given, that is, the conditions that are imposed by the subject himself. These conditions are nothing but categorial principles, which are subjective in origin. The sensible manifolds are given under the categorial conditions imposed by the knowing mind. And finally nothing can be given to knowing mind beyond sensible manifolds conditioned by the subject.

But in Scheler's scheme, if anything is to be given to the knowing mind, it is given under no conditions. The given, in Scheler's view, is something which is objective in character and also something non-sensible in nature. The intentional acts of knowing consciousness is directed towards it to have it in consciousness but in no way determined by it. So what is given to knowing subject is given as it is, that is, under *no* conditions. Thus Scheler's conception of the "given", unlike that of Kant, is free from subjective influence.

Further, on Kant's view, the *a priori* fastens itself with propositions as pure forms of judgments, as he believes that the synthesizing function of the understanding that constitutes objects for us by combining and relating the ultimate data of sense is one with the function of judgment. As we know, for Kant, all knowledge is judgemental in nature. But, for Scheler, *a priori* belongs to the given, to the realm of "facts" and *not* to the sphere of judgment or "thought". Scheler rejects that the epistemological doctrines that presuppose that a factor in cognition *must* be *either* sensible *or* "thought" is a great obstruction to formulate a theory of cognition based on non-sensible intuition. For, on the basis of this presupposition, one is unable to bring to fulfillment the concepts like force, motion, equality, space, time, values etc. On Scheler's view, there must be a *datum* of non-sensible intuition for them, which provides the basis for cognition that is *a priori* in character. If the datum or the fundamental factor is *not* there then these concepts would be "fabricated," that is, "posited out of nothingness by 'thinking'."[11] Or if this datum is taken to be of sensible character, then content would be subjective and relative to the psychophysical organization of man. And consequently, cognition is destined to have *no* content, which is of *a priori* nature but consists only of logical factors.

Thus the coincidence of *a priori* with the logical factors, Scheler points out, is detrimental particularly to ethics. In keeping with the traditional dichotomy between reason and sensibility, Kant takes side with the logical aspect of human spirit and identifies pure willing with practical reason. Thus the sphere of willing is taken by Kant to be an area of application for logic. This Kantian move, according to Scheler, misconceives the *originality* of the act of willing, as having its own *a priori* lawfulness, which is not borrowed from "thinking". For Scheler, the structure of the act of willing is entirely independent of logic on which an *a priori* ethics can very well be founded. In other words, according to Scheler, our emotional aspect of mind is not totally chaotic and disorderly. Rather, it contains a logic or reason of its own, which is cognitive in nature. This emotional-cognitive aspect of our mind makes our ethical knowledge possible and hence an ethics which can claim to be both absolute *and* a priori.

3. For Kant, *necessity* and *universality* are the two essential marks of the *a priori*. But Scheler needs *no* such marks for his conception of a priori. According to Scheler, necessity first of all pertains solely to the propositions (e.g., the relation between premise and conclusion) and not to facts of *intuition* except derivatively. And secondly, necessity, for Scheler, is a *negative* concept in the sense that its opposite is impossible. Scheler talks of *a priori insight* and *not* of *a priori* proposition. It is an *insight* into the essential state-of-affairs and first given not in judgment but in *intuition.* And it is, unlike that of Kant's, a *positive* concept in the sense that it is an insight into the "factual" state-of-affairs. Scheler says,

> Whenever we speak of "necessity," we must presuppose as *true* those propositions *according* to which propositional relations are necessary … . But it is clear that *these* propositions and their *truth* cannot be reduced to any "necessity" that would differ from mere "mental constraint." They are *true because they are a priori evident*. It is because the being of something contradicts its non-being in intuition that the above proposition is true.[12]

According to Scheler, the *a priori* is not founded on necessity but rather the latter is founded upon the former. That is, a logical proposition derives its necessity from the *a priori* intuition and not *vice versa*. This conception of *a priori* holds equally true, for

Scheler, in the domain of values and ethics. The "necessity of oughtness" is founded upon the *insight* into *a priori* connections among values. The necessity of ought and the judgments has its foundation in the insight into *a priori* structure of values and not *vice versa.*

4. Universality too, for Scheler, has nothing to do with the *a priori*. Nor does it in any sense belong to the nature of essence. An essence or whatness as such is neither universal nor particular. The essence "red", for example, is neither universal nor particular except when it is considered in the context of plurality of different objects as an identical essence or in relation to an individual thing. This, however, is not to deny the proposition of formal logic such as the law of contradiction as universally applicable. In fact, Scheler denies those propositions that are grounded on the operation of understanding as Kant thinks. Thus, Scheler writes,

> ... universality in the sense of a validity "for" all subjects having a certain "understanding," or for the human species, has nothing to do with the "a priori." There can very well be an a priori for only *one* individual's insight, or one that only one individual *can* have! A proposition based on the a priori is "universal" only for those subjects who *can* have the same insight (all universality is essentially "for" someone, whereas the a priori does not at all imply such a "for" relation).[13]

Scheler's point is that both universal and individual essences are *equally* valid from phenomenological perspective. They *become* universal or particular when they are intuited by subjects. A proposition founded on an *a priori* essence becomes universal by virtue of being identical intuition of all subjects.

5. Scheler rejects the Kantian attempt to make "a priori" *understandable* or even to "explain" it. Kant attempts to "explain" the *a priori* by means of his theory of "spontaneity" of thinking according to which the manifold of sensations given to sensibility through *a priori* form of space and time are in need of order and connection. This act of combining and relating, called synthesis, is credited to the understanding, which imposes a *formal* structure upon the manifold of sensations and thereby makes knowledge

possible. Every phenomenon is thus necessarily a "product" of spontaneous and synthetic activity of the understanding. In Kantian scheme, this theory of synthetic activity is so closely interwoven with his conception of *a priori* that his readers, according to Scheler, consider the two as constituting an inseparable whole. "But", Scheler argues,

> this mythology of productive rational activity has nothing to do with apriorism; it does not rest on intuition, but is a *purely constructivistic explanation* of the a priori contents of objects of experience, an explanation based on the very *presupposition* that only a "disordered chaos" is "given" (on the one hand, so-called sensations; on the other, "drives" or "inclinations").[14]

In other words, Scheler rejects the Kantian distinction between the "spontaneity" of thought and "receptivity" of sensibility as an unjustifiable means of trying to *explain* the *a priori*. This is purely *constructivistic* approach to *a priori*, which is unacceptable to Scheler.

Kant's attempt to "explain" the *a priori*, according to Scheler, is rooted in his baseless fear that the "objects" or the "givens," if not made amenable to our rational laws of thinking, experiencing, remembering etc. would remain a bundle of chaos. Scheler further points out that Kant's notion of *a priori* is conjoined with his deep-rooted personal attitude towards the world in general. Alfred Schutz writes on behalf of Scheler:

> In general, Kant's attitude toward the world can only be characterized as hostility to and distrust of everything that is "given," as dread of the chaos he considers the external world and internal nature to be: both have to be formed, organized, dominated by understanding and reason and by reason-guided volition in order to make them safe by putting them straight. This attitude is the opposite to love of the world, to trusting it, to surrendering to it in affectionate vision. Expressed by a philosophical genius, it is the way in which modern man faces the world.[15]

Thus, it becomes clear as to how the crucial notion of *a priori* bifurcates the respective conception of experience developed by Kant and Scheler.

3. Critique of the Kantian Intellectualism

In his theory of knowledge, Kant's assumes that what is given to sense-intuition through universal forms of space and time is something unruly and confused elements. They are in need of synthesis by understanding or thought under its own *a priori* concepts or categories in order to be a piece of knowledge. In his ethics, on the other hand, Kant takes for granted that human inclinations are in a state of complete chaos and that these too are in need of some *a priori* order to be bestowed upon them. This order-conferring function is entrusted by Kant to the *rational* subject. According to Kant, the rational order is the only order that is contributed by the rational will or practical reason. Also for Kant, the ethical discernment, that is, the apprehension of the moral law or the imperative is possible only by self-legislating Reason. Since the moral law or the Categorical Imperative is, for Kant, a "fact of pure reason", in the sense that it is always expressed in the form of a judgment, it is the function of none other than Reason to grasp it.

However, the role of moral feeling has not been totally denied by Kant in his ethics. He talks of feeling of *respect* (Achtung) for the moral law. We find only oblique references of feeling of respect in Kant's writings where he recognizes that feeling of respect is a kind of non-sensible feeling – "a spiritual feeling 'effected by the moral law'."[16] According to Scheler, Kant considers all morally relevant feelings to be of sensible origin except the feeling of respect. Although Kant provides the feeling of respect a place in his ethics, he, on Scheler's view, still sticks to his rational approach to morality. As for Kant, Scheler writes,

> ... only a formal ethics, which, as a rational ethics, eschews all references to the emotive life, can avoid those errors to which all imaginable forms of eudaemonism lead (...).[17]

Kant's adherence to rationalism and formalism, according to Scheler, is because of his "*impoverished*" view of man's emotional life and of his conception of value. For him, human beings naturally strive for pleasure when he is not guided by his rational will, by the moral law. This conception of Kant coincides with eudaemonistic or more basically, with hedonistic conception of man. The only way, for Kant, to salvage human beings from the cesspool of sensualism is to bind them under rational and formal law. That is, man is needed to be determined, not by his natural inclinations, but by something beyond it – by his self-legislating Reason.

Now, Scheler points out that Kant is wrong in supposing that moral experience possesses *no* other order than the rational one; that there is no other insight than the *rational* insight. Because of his impoverished view of man's emotive life, he fails to see the richness and orderliness contained in it. Hence, he embraces the dualistic framework of Reason and Sensibility. For, according to this tradition, everything that is not rational must be assigned to sensibility. As consequence of upholding this division between reason and sensibility, ethical theories since ancient times down to the present era have been formulated either as rational, and therefore absolute and *a priori* or as non-rational, i.e., emotional, and therefore relative and *a posteriori*. That it is possible to build an edifice of ethics, which is both absolute yet affective, has seldom been considered.

Again, in keeping with this tradition, according to Scheler, Kant has placed the emotional content of our spirit such as feeling, preferring, loving and hating to the sensible sphere. As for him, there is no lawfulness and orderliness in them in order to be a mode of moral experience. Scheler, on the contrary, argues that there *is* a spiritual level of our cognition for evaluating goods and actions which has nothing to do with the sphere of the sensible or the pure laws of thought. Scheler discovers an order of cognition in human *emotion* as an alternative to the Kantian rational order, which enables us to discover "moral facts". He undertakes a thorough analysis of cognitive emotions or what he calls feeling-acts in which values or moral facts are given both in non-logical yet non-sensible manner. Unlike Kant, Scheler considers reason as a cognitive faculty, which is not a source of *moral* experience. The gulf between Kantian and Schelerian conceptions of cognition has vividly been brought out by Ronald Perrin in the following manner:

> In the Kantian view, experience is a synthetic construction designed and carried out by thought. Hence, whoever would understand the order we find in the world must begin by describing the nature of thought. For Scheler, this is an approach that conceals more than it reveals. In the end such an effort must become entrapped in a massive 'symbolism' that is, at best, a reflection of reality. The truth is better served by attending closely and faithfully to what is given *to* consciousness, rather than by dwelling upon the internal processes of the rational consciousness themselves. For Kant the idea of a pre-conceptual experience is profoundly mystifying; for Scheler it is reality itself.[18]

However, Scheler does not deny that there is a rational procedure of knowledge, and this is, for Scheler, not the *only* procedure. His point is that our emotional aspect of mind is equally capable of making a claim to be another order of reason, which is, in Pascal's terms, the "logic of heart".

Notes

1. Frings, M.S. & Funk, R.L. "Foreword" to the English translation of *Formalism in Ethics,* op. cit. p. 15.
2. Scheler, M. *Formalism in Ethics*, op. cit. p. 9.
3. Ibid., p. 10.
4. Scheler substantiates his point by quoting the first Theorem of the *Critique of Practical Reason:* "All practical principles which presuppose an *object* (material) of the faculty of desire as the determining ground of the will are, without exception, empirical and can furnish no practical laws. By 'material of the faculty of desire' I mean an object whose reality is desired", See, *Formalism in Ethics,* p. 11.
5. Perrin, R. *Max Scheler's Concept of the Person: An Ethics of Humanism,* (Macmillan, Hong Kong, 1991), p. 54.
6. Scheler, M. *Formalism in Ethics,* op. cit. p. 47.
7. Ibid., p. 48.
8. Ibid., p. 54.
9. Ibid., p. 55.

10. Mall, R.A. "Husserl's Criticism of Kant's Theory of Knowledge," *The Journal of the Indian Academy of Philosophy*, Vol. VI, No. I, May 1967, p. 30-31.
11. Scheler, M. *Formalism in Ethics*, p. 63.
12. Ibid., p. 74-75.
13. Ibid., p. 76.
14. Ibid., p. 66.
15. Schutz, A. "Max Scheler's Epistemology and Ethics", *Collected Papers III*, (Martinus Nijhoff, The Hague, 1975), p. 156.
16. Scheler, M. *Formalism in Ethics*, op. cit. p. 241.
17. Ibid., p. 239.
18. Perrin, R. *Max Scheler's Concept of the Person: An Ethics of Humanism*, op. cit. p. 64.

5

Hartmann's Value-Platonism

Hartmann is regarded as a philosopher who belongs to the Platonic tradition,[1] though he combines well with it some basic phenomenological insights. Quite avowedly, he builds his philosophical theories on the Platonic structure of thinking. And, his ethical theory is not an exception to this. Hartmann relates his philosophy of value to what may be considered as Platonic foundations. Hartmann harks back to the Platonic notion of Ideas and establishes his theory of moral values on it. Plato conceives of a realm of Being, namely, "the realm of Ideas", other than the domain of the phenomenal world. Hartmann finds this Platonic conception to be illuminating for his theory of value. This is evident from his following statement:

> Characteristically among Plato's ideas are found ethical principles, the ideal "virtue" – those values upon which his ethics was built. This fact is especially illuminating for the theory of value: in their mode of Being, values are Platonic ideas.[2]

However, it should be kept in mind that Hartmann's concern is not the Platonic theory of Ideas in general but with *some aspects* of this theory. Hartmann advocates in his theory of value what is called "value-Platonism", and this may be defined as follows: Value-Platonism is a philosophical position according to which there are entities, called values, which are "real" and form an objective realm of their own *apart* from the spatio-temporal world. Like Platonism itself, Value-Platonism historically takes on various forms, and this has given rise to a good deal of confusion.

However, we propose presently to discuss the value-Platonism as adumbrated by Nicolai Hartmann in his *Ethics*.

The term "value" has been used in Hartmann's value-Platonism in a definite sense, and it requires us to make a distinction between a *thing* or *event*, which is to be judged valuable (e.g., good, right, etc.) and the *standard* or *norm* according to which it is judged to be valuable. The distinction here is between the *items* as evaluated and *in virtue of* which a thing or event is evaluated. Cadwallader[3] has used the term "actualized-value" for the former and "value-ideal" for the latter. Now, actualized-values are *in time* and they are part of history. They are actual entities considered in their aspect of having been valued by some subject. But, on the other hand, value-ideals are *not* in space and time, and therefore, they are not the sort of things that are in or of the *natural* world at all. They belong to the *ideal* order of being. Further, actualized values are dependent on the person, thing or relation to which they are thought to be attached. However, the value-ideals are totally independent of any person, thing or relation whatsoever. Thus, the term "value" in Hartmann's value-Platonism means *value-ideal* as distinguished from the value that is actualized.

Hartmann seems to have inherited the following leading ideas from Plato:

1. Values represent a world of their own, like Plato's Ideas, *detached* from the mundane world. This means that values have a peculiar *mode of being,* like those of Plato's Ideas and unlike the objects of mundane reality having spatio-temporal existence. Quite in the way of Plato's conception of Ideas as Ideal Being, Hartmann gives values the status of *ideal* Beings. To have his own words, "in their mode of Being, values are Platonic ideas". Hartmann's focus of interest here is on Plato's theory of Ideal Being.

2. A notion of "ground" is attached to Plato's Ideas as essences, in the sense that Ideas are Ideal Form, and participating in which an object becomes a real object. That is to say, Ideas are that "through which" everything that participates in them gets its foundation as an object. This notion of "ground" has been duly taken note of and emphasized by Hartmann. According to

Hartmann, "they (values) are that 'through which' everything which participates in them is exactly as it is – namely valuable."[4] In other words, "... real things have value through partaking in the ideal Forms which are values."[5]

3. Hartmann also takes over the Platonic notion of *apriorism*. According to Plato, Ideas are *a priori* to all existing things and beings in the sense that they are intuited *independently* of all things and beings. For Hartmann, "The Platonic philosophy is the historical discovery of the *aprioristic* element in the whole realm of human knowledge."[6] Further, ethical values cannot be discovered in the conduct of man as "Values are not to be recognized by the fact that they are, or are not, contained in the real."[7] Values are given *a priori*, and like Plato's Ideas, "... they are not even capable of being directly grasped by thought; rather are they immediately discerned only by an inner 'vision,' like Plato's 'Ideas.'"[8]

4. Values, much as Plato's Ideas, are many and *not* one. They are independent of all other actual and possible worlds as also of one another. They constitute a world of plural units something that is like Plato's ideal Forms. Hartmann also employs the Platonic conception of dual world, that is, the world of Ideas and the world of things and beings. As for Hartmann, there is an *ideal realm* for values to subsist on the one hand and the spatio-temporal world where they actually occur, on the other.

5. The term "a priori" in respect of knowledge of values must be understood here in the sense that such "... apriority of the knowledge of them is no intellectual or reflective apriority, but is emotional, intuitive."[9] As for Hartmann, "The Platonic notion of 'beholding' well fits that which material ethics designates as the 'sensing of value,' that which is embodied in acts of preference, of approval, of conviction."[10] Let us now turn to Hartmann's characterization of values.

1. Values as "Independent" Mode of Beings

Before we have Hartmann's positive characterization of values, we may begin by making some clarificatory remarks so as to avoid certain possible confusions. In the first place, values do not reside in valuable things. Nor are they discerned in things that are valuable. They also do not emanate from the valuable objects. Further, quite obviously, values are different from the natural objects and they cannot be defined or experienced in naturalistic terms. Values cannot be defined with reference to the subject's specific mental attitudes. Moreover, values arise neither with our desires, nor with our interest in them. In a word, values are not the product of subjectivism and psychologism.

We have already taken note of Plato's theory about objectively existing and most real entities (i.e., Ideas) and how it was inherited by Hartmann. What is distinctive, for Hartmann, about Platonic Ideas is that they are *not* in the actual world, in space and time. So, for Hartmann, values are radically different sort of things, belonging to a different type of "world"; their mode of being is *unique*. Hartmann conceives them as having the *same mode* like that of Ideas. Values have their place in an ideal world of Being, *independent* of spatio-temporality. Further, like Platonic Ideas, values are real, and therefore, they are not something fictitious. Their mode of being is very much like the physical objects, in the sense that they cannot be imagined away or wished away by the will of the subject; the only *difference* being that values *lack* spatio-temporality.

According to Hartmann, values are not only "real" but they are *independently* "real". They do not depend on anything else other than themselves for their "existence". They are also independent of each other. As for Hartmann, "... there is a realm of values subsisting for itself."[11] That is, "Values have self-existence."[12] He defines "self-existence" thus:

> Whatever in its mode of being is not relative to a subject, whatever confronts a thinking subject as independent and immovable, whatever sets us before him a self-subsistent regularity and energy of its own which the subject can grasp or miss but cannot get rid of, that has for him the character of self-existence.[13]

Here we have three important ideas: (i) the mode of being of values is independent of persons; (ii) they stand differently to persons as static; and (iii) values have their own uniformity and energy which a person may or may not be able to grasp, but cannot get rid of.

In order to understand the above-mentioned ideas in relation to values, it is necessary to explain the distinction, which Hartmann makes, between the content and the valuational character. We have already pointed out that the values are not formal empty structures, but are "material" structures for having their contents. This content is different from the valuational character, though the latter inheres in the former. In other words, it is content or "material", which has value inherent in itself. Hartmann clarifies, "The content and the valuational character do not coincide."[14] Although the "material" or content is always different from the valuableness, they are not unrelated to each other. The valuableness varies with its material. For example, the material essence of trust is different from that of fidelity, so it's valuational character. "And, nevertheless," Hartmann says,

> valuableness is a something which through all differentiations always remains different from the material; a something which builds above it, camps over it, lends to it a glimmer of meaning, a significance of a higher order, an import which for ever remains transcendent to the existential reality; a something which remains on the further side of reality, incomparable, and which always draws it into another sphere of cohesions, into the intelligible order of values.[15]

Let us now relate this distinction to the above-mentioned three points which, according to Hartmann, constitute the self-existent character of values. Firstly, it is valuableness and *not* the material, which is *independent* of the subject who passes the moral judgment, and independent of the judgment itself. It is also independent of subject's actual conduct. It is not the product of subject's biological or psychological process. Thus, the being of valuableness remains independent of person, although it remains "behind" all actions of the person to make them valuable or it's opposite. Secondly, it is again *not* the material but the valuableness or value-ideal, which stands opposite to the person as *static* and *unchangeable*. It "exists" *independently* of whether one knows them or not. That is to say, awareness or non-awareness of them by a subject does *not* affect their own "self-existent reality". As it is clear from Hartmann's following statement:

> Values subsist independently of the consciousness of them. Consciousness can grasp or miss them, but cannot make them or spontaneously decree them.[16]

Thirdly, the value-ideal has its own regularity and energy, which the subject can apprehend or miss, but cannot free himself from. A subject can very well produce a "material", e.g., he can set up a relation of confidence with other person. However, once he produces such a material, he cannot prevent the material to be something of value. A material, (here, the relation of confidence) once produced, needs no co-operation from the subject to be something of value and the *vice versa*. Such a "material" subsists with *no* co-operation from any quarter. A subject may produce a "material" and he may believe that it is devoid of moral worth. However, the *belief* does not affect the value which inheres in the "material" or content. In fact, for Hartmann, the "Knowledge of values is genuine knowledge of Being."[17]

Further, this knowledge of values, according to Hartmann, is primarily *emotional* which Hartmann calls "sensing of value"[18] or "feeling of value".[19] In valuational vision and feeling, the willing subject remains purely receptive. He cannot get rid of the appeal that values make upon him. He is disposed to have the primary sensing of value when he produces a "material". The moral consciousness cannot reject the appeal of values made upon it through *feeling*. In other words, the Being of value, the object, determines the consciousness, the subject through the "primary discovery"[20] of them but not *vice versa*. As Hartmann puts it:

> In this 'beholding' of them the subject is purely receptive; he surrenders himself to them. He sees himself determined by the object, the self-existent value; but he himself, on his side, determines nothing.[21]

Our discussion, so far, of self-existence of values centres round the meaning of self-existence *for knowledge*. However, ethics, as Hartmann points out, is not concerned with the knowledge of values *alone* but with the *values themselves*, i.e., with the *mode* of values. So, let us now turn to a consideration of as to how the values are *self-existent* from the point of view of ontology.

According to Hartmann, values do not have self-existence as that which belongs to all things and events, to whatever has spatio-temporal existence. "Values have no self-existence that is real."[22] Values, on the other hand, belong to an *ideal* order of being and therefore, they are themselves ideal beings. Values, for having their characteristic nature, have self-existence that is *ideal*. As Hartmann says, "The mode of Being peculiar to values is evidently that of an *ideal* self-existence."[23] They have their own regularity, laws and order which constitute their ideal nature. As principles of action, values' participation, in determining the reality in specific ways, does not affect their *ideal* mode of self-existence. As valuational quality of a specific material, (e.g., sincerity) remains in ideal mode as an essence, whether it is embodied in someone's conduct or not. In its ideal mode, valuational quality is independent, and therefore, self-subsistent. It must be noted that the "actualized" value, e.g., the sincerity embodied in the conduct of someone is indeed a value, but only a *derived* one. These actualized values are merely "Ideas" whose root lies in the value of the material. Hartmann goes so far as to say that "Strictly taken, values themselves are not at all 'actualized,' but only the materials, to which, whether ideal or real, the value belongs."[24]

Further, Hartmann compares the mode of being of values with logico-mathematical "objects" as he thinks that values and the logico-mathematical "objects" stand on the *same* ontological footing. Hartmann writes,

> As regards the mode of Being peculiar to values, nothing is so instructive as its close analogy to the *theoretical essences*, especially to the mathematical and logical structures.[25]

Elsewhere,[26] he says that the sphere of values are connected organically with the sphere of logico-mathematical objects, and the former sphere is the "continuation" of the latter; the only difference being that "Pure logic, pure mathematics and the essences are theoretical idealities while the values are axiological idealities."[27]

2. Values as *A priori*

Values, according to Hartmann, are *a priori*. A value, for Hartmann, is a "conditioning factor". As Hartmann puts it:

"Indeed, it [value] must be an *a priori* condition."[28] Now it is necessary to understand what Hartmann means by the term, "a priori". It seems that there are two ideas that are conjoined here: (i) that which is "independent of experience"[29] and (ii) that which is "already presupposed."[30] Let us take each one at a time. If x is something that exists/subsists *independently* of some experience called y, but y cannot exist without x, then this implies that x has *independent* ontological status. Now for (ii): If something x is presupposed by some experience y, then x is the conditional factor for some experience y. Thus, "Hartmann uses the term 'a priori' to mean 'both epistemologically and ontologically prior.'"[31] But, for Hartmann, to show that y cannot exist or subsist without the existence/subsistence of x is to "know" x *a priori.* Thus Hartmann expresses the meaning of "a priori" in the Kantian phrase, which is referred to as the "conditions of the possibility."[32] What it means is that values are presupposed in all the phenomena of value-experience. To the question, what are necessary conditions of the possibility of something to be valuable? Hartmann's answer would be that

> "... values are a conditioning *prius* of all phenomena of the moral life, in connection with which the apriority of the valuational consciousness constitutes only one partial phenomenon."[33]

Values are a *condition* of the possibility of goods, persons or conduct. To put the matter differently as Hartmann does, "... they [values] are that through which things are valuable."[34] Not only this. Hartmann further maintains that "Values are not only conditions of the possibility of goods, but are also conditions of all ethical phenomena in general."[35] To our understanding, it seems that Hartmann generally combines all of the following when he states that values are *a priori*:

1. In order for something to exist, a value must already pre-exist.

2. In order for us to know something to be valuable, a value must be *believed* to have existence beforehand.

3. In order for something to be valuable, a value is a *necessary condition*.

We may stress here the point that all of the above senses of *a priori* unilaterally mean that values are *a priori with respect to* our experience of valuable things. That is, the value-ideals are prior to what we have called "actualized values". For example, if something x is a value-ideal, then it exists independently *prior* to actualized value y. What needs to be noted is that this priority is *not* temporal, but logical.

Now, to recapitulate briefly the point of our preceding discussion, it may be said that in Hartmann's view, in knowing something to be valuable, one will have to presuppose the standard through which he "feels" a thing to be something of value. But one may say, by way of objection, that we find values in the nature of abstractions from something that is valuable. How would Hartmann respond to this objection? It seems, Hartmann would then reply by saying that in order to have experience of something valuable, one must first logically *presuppose* that there subsists a value-ideal by reference to which one "feels" something to be valuable. In Hartmann's words,

> [One] must possess beforehand the standard; for example, the standard of the pleasant and the unpleasant, and from the start things must fall for him under this standard, they must divide themselves according to it into things pleasant and unpleasant.[36]

In other words, one becomes able to make the distinction between good and evil, pleasant and unpleasant only because one is possessed of a standard. The sense of value or standard prepares one to tell a certain thing either as good or bad.

Before we turn to the *arguments* in support of this view, it may be well to take note of a more clear articulation of the point in the following:

> ... a thing can be valuable only through its relation to a value itself. This must be fixed beforehand. It is the *condition of the possibility* of there being anything of value and of its being recognized as valuable, as a good – so to speak. Nothing is ever loved, striven for, yearned after, except for the sake of some value immediately discerned (and felt).[37]

A thing, person or deed must have reference to a value in order to be something of value. A value must be *immediately* discovered in order something to be called goods. A value is always presupposed in the case of a thing or conduct that is of value. This relation to values with the things that are valuable is irreversible. "It is essentially a one-sided dependence."[38] What is called "actualized value" is always dependent upon a value-ideal to be something of value but not *vice versa*.

We shall now turn to the *arguments* in support of the view that values are *a priori*. Let us state them systematically in terms of the following points:

1. Hartmann begins by asking the question, viz., "what is experience of goods?" To this, his answer is, "It is something a priori."[39] To put the matter pointedly: In our experience of a thing as useful, serviceable, etc., the *knowledge of value* of usefulness or serviceability is assumed *beforehand*. Here the value, namely, usefulness or serviceability, is *felt* to be already *fixed*. This feeling of fixity of value beforehand implies that they (i.e., value-ideals) are *a priori*.

2. The second argument may also be put in terms of a question: why a certain thing is good? The answer to this may be that it is good for some *other* thing, which will be the same question, why that other thing is good? Evidently, an unending circle of back-reference will lead us to a vicious epistemological regress. In order to escape from this circle of back-reference, one has to answer this question by reference to a *value* which first converts a thing into a valuable thing. So Hartmann argues, "It [the circle of back-reference] does not come to a rest until one no longer answers with a good but with a value – that is, with what first converts things in general into goods."[40] The crux of the matter is that the intelligibility of certain value-experience is made possible only by means of a self-subsistent value-ideal existing "behind" actualized values.

3. For the next move in the argument, consider the fact that every one of us is doing this or that work in our life. However, to the question, "what are we working for?" the answer must be with reference to a value. A life is worth living for having a value attached to it. "But", for Hartmann,

> therein is conceded the apriorical reference of work to a value striven for; in this case the reference is to a value higher than that of life itself, a value which alone makes life "valuable" and gives meaning to work. Only here does it become quite evident that appraisement of value precedes experience. For that which is striven for is still unreal, at least not yet "experienced."[41]

4. Values, according to Hartmann, are pre-requisite of all ethical phenomena. The object of volition has the form of an end, and the end can never be contentless. If there is nothing valuable in the content of an end, it would be impossible to adopt anything as an end. However, this content or valuational character needs not be known clearly. The valuational consciousness must possess a "sense" of its quality as a value. As Hartmann points out, "Values are not only conditions of the possibility of goods, but also conditions of all ethical phenomena in general."[42] The point of the matter is that a value *precedes* the experience of all ethical phenomena.

5. For another turn of argument, Hartmann considers the following situation: A subordinate person carries out the orders of his boss, even though he does not know the end of his boss's orders. That is to say, he does not know the value or aim which guides his boss to issue the order to him. In this case, the content of the command is the ultimate value to him. The subordinate believes in it, though he cannot "see" it. In this belief inheres the moral value of *obedience*. "The authoritative command (of the boss) which is taken up uncritically, and the *independently discerned value* which determines the end, are both equally a priori ... ."[43]

6. And finally, Hartmann cites the case of choosing an exemplar in moral, religious or political life to prove that the values are *a priori*. Suppose that I choose Mahatma Gandhi as a model; this is certainly not an accidental matter but has a definite ground. This ground, according to Hartmann, is valuational. It is possible that Mahatma Gandhi as a pattern of my moral life meets certain moral qualities which I like to have or satisfy me by its value-content. This satisfaction provided by Mahatma Gandhi as a pattern of my moral life consists in its coincidence with the

standards which I consciously or unconsciously cherish. The setting up of Mahatma Gandhi as a model is consequent upon a moral judgment passed on him as a value. But here values are not abstracted from the model. Rather conversely, it is my *a priori discernment* of values, which guides me to choose Mahatma Gandhi as model of my life. Hence,

> The intuitive, emotionally toned knowledge of what a model ought to be is as such a function of the primary sense of values. Here also the values are the *prius*, the conditioning factor. The consciousness of what is worthy of imitation is nothing except a form of the aprioristic consciousness of value.[44]

To summarize the points, the factor which decides whether a conduct is good or not does not reside in the conduct itself or in its sphere upon which a moral judgment is passed. This deciding factor is self-dependent and *a priori*. Thus in all kinds of striving, of yearning after something, a value is always presupposed. A value, therefore, is not dependent upon things that are valuable, nor do they lie within the sphere of actions. Rather, the things and actions are dependent upon the value-ideals in order to be something of value; hence the apriority of values.

Before bringing the section to a close, it may be reiterated that, for Hartmann, values are not formal *a priori* but are "material" *a priori*. They are not empty structures, but are possessed of contents, which form the specific quality of things, actions, etc. In Hartmann's words,

> ... they (values) are "materials," structures which constitute a specific quality of things, relations or persons according as they attach to them or are lacking.[45]

The concept of "material a priori" is of fundamental importance in Hartmann's ethics, and this very concept is at the root of his formulation of material ethics as against Kantian formal ethics.

3. Values as Absolute

As values are not part of the physical world, one may even suspect that they are something subjective. A thing or action may be said to have a value only for someone who values them. Appraisement of a thing or an action exists only in human consciousness, and therefore, one may conclude that values exist only for a human consciousness, only for the one who discerns them. And ultimately this view leads one to admit that the mode of being of values is relative. But this position seems to be inconsistent with Hartmann's general standpoint with regard to values. As for him,

> These [values] themselves have an existential character. They by no means subsist only for the one who discerns them, but in themselves. We come upon them and can in no way dispose of them at will; they are not relative to a consciousness of phenomena, but subsist independently of it, and by the philosophical consciousness itself are deemed to be independent of it.[46]

In other words, values are absolute. Absoluteness, for Hartmann, is "the kind of Being peculiar to values."[47] To put it differently, values that belong to the self-subsistent order of being have their *own* kind of reality. To clarify this point, a brief discussion on the relation of goods to the subject will be quite in order.

It is true that a personal subject has to unconditionally accept what is good for him as good and what is bad for him as bad. It is not within his power to change a thing which is good or bad for him. The fact is that a man has his power, to some extent, to strive for something which for him is good and avoid something which for him is an evil. Here, obviously, a kind of relatedness of goods to the person is given. While the "relatedness" implies that the values are applicable to person, from this it does not follow that values themselves are relative. Here the subject does not have an *active* role, that is, to determine the values. Hartmann takes up the examples of geometrical laws and psychological laws which hold good unconditionally for spatio-temporal figures and psychic beings respectively. *This* does not mean that the laws themselves are always absolute. Rather, the spatial figures and psychic beings are unconditionally subjected to the laws of geometry and psychology respectively. Similarly, according to Hartmann, the consciousness of good and evil is subject unconditionally to the valuational or anti-valuational laws. "In short", Hartmann concludes,

> the relatedness of these values to a human subject is not relativity to the subject's opinion of them or to his appraisement of them, but to the subject's existence, including his entire categorial constitution.[48]

Let us consider those values that adhere, not to things, but to the action, to the disposition and will. These values, as determining *prius,* control human actions. Approving or disapproving of human conduct presupposes a value. It is value that determines/controls man. Values are always *fixed beforehand.* These values do not have existence "for" the subject who values them, like those of goods-values. Here the moral worth of a person's conduct does not lie in being valuable "for" another person but simply for having a moral quality in the conduct. "In their material", Hartmann points out,

> there is no essential or necessary "existence for me" which would be included as an objective relation in the structure of its self-existence. Moral values have another kind of autonomy, evidently more absolute.[49]

Now it is interesting to note that Hartmann distinguishes three possible kinds of relatedness of value, which may apparently be regarded *as* implying the relativity of moral values. Let us mark them off, clearly.

1. To begin with, Hartmann explains that a moral value *seems* to be relative when it turns out be a goods-value to another. For example, trust is good thing for one to whom it is shown. Thus, the relation of trust becomes a goods-value to a person to whom it is shown. However, Hartmann points out that the moral worth of a person does not lie in being precious thing to another person. The moral value (here, trust) inheres in him even if it is not good "for" anyone. It remains exclusively as a quality of his own conduct. As Hartmann writes,

> ... it subsists exclusively as a quality of his own personality, of his own conduct as such. It is fundamentally a different value from that which accompanies it when it is good for another. And the appraisement of it, which the moral judgment makes, is independent of value set upon the benefit which it confers upon another person.[50]

Now, this relatedness to another person as a goods-value, Hartmann points out, does not in any way mean a valuational relativity. For moral judgment is passed not on being a goods-value to another person, but on the person who possesses the moral value in question in his own conduct.

2. Second, moral values are values of *dispositions*, which are always towards some person. The object of moral value is the *person* and *not* the things. The relation of the value to other person inheres in the structure of the content of moral values, which is quite different from the goods-value that goes with it. Here, we find two kinds of relationality, which are dependent on each other: (a) when, for example, fidelity is practiced towards other person, the latter feels a sense of security, and becomes able to entrust himself to the faithful person. This is goods-value to him. And (b) the moral value of trust possessed by the trusted person consists in spiritual strength, trustworthiness, etc. which themselves are values. These two kinds of value do not coincide. Similarly, the two kinds of underlying relationships are also radically different. In the case of fidelity, the conduct of the other person towards whom it is practiced is conditioned by the act of the trusted person. Hartmann thereby concludes, "The inner, intentional relatedness conditions the outer relationality of the goods-value which is dependent upon it."[51] But these two kinds of relationality do not in any way mean valuational relativity.

3. A third kind of relationality is as follows. This is between *value* and the *bearer* of value. Here the bearer of value is a personal subject who can will, sets up ends, pursues them, has the ability to feel the value, and is capable of human conduct. Such a person is the moral subject. A moral value is attached to his complete categorial constitution, to his personality as a whole and not merely to his particular acts. A moral person stands "behind" all of his acts. He may be praised for his certain conduct and/or may be blamed for others. Even the contradictory value qualities may be conferred on him. All these touch the essence of his moral person. As Hartmann summaries,

> All moral imputations attach to the person, he bears the guilt and responsibility; judgments of approval and disapproval made by others, as well as condemnation through his own conscience, apply to him as a person. In this way moral values are related to the person as a carrier of values.[52]

However, Hartmann points out that the relation of moral value to its bearer, that is, moral person is merely a kind of *relationality* and does *not* in any way mean the valuational *relativity*. For the relatedness of moral value to the person as its bearer is not dependent on the person who *thinks* that certain moral dispositions exists. It is rather a moral value, which has universal character. The relation of moral value to the person as a bearer inheres in the material and not in the moral value itself. The relatedness of moral values to its bearer, therefore, does not mean valuational relativity.

What Hartmann needs stressing here is that the relationality and relativity of values are two *different* things. According to Hartmann, values can be relational without being relative. In other words, they can be relational yet remaining absolute. The relationality of values with whatever else does not affect the absoluteness of them. The relationality of values does not imply that their independence can be questioned. In fact, values cannot but be relational; or else valuing would be impossible. For Hartmann, therefore, the absoluteness of values comes to mean that they are not relative to anything else. The opposite of relativity means the absoluteness of values. If they were so, then our talk of normative discourse could not make any sense at all.

4. Values as Principles

In Hartmann's view, "Values are also principles."[53] First, values are principles of the *ideal* ethical sphere. The material content of values is purely ideal in nature, and its fulfilment in the real is merely accidental. This is in no way necessitated by the ideal content as principle. The ideal content of values is "felt" to be something independent of reality and of actualization. For Hartmann,

> Values are primarily and throughout *ideal* self-existents; in so far as they are principles, they are from beginning to end only principles of the ethical *ideal* sphere.[54]

According to Hartmann, the being of ideal sphere and the being of principle are different. For, the ideal sphere of values contains, in addition to independent values, what are called *derivative* values, such as, the value of useful, mediating values which are also *ideal* but they cannot claim themselves to be principles. "Genuine, proper values, however, are *principles* of the ethical ideal sphere."[55]

Secondly, ethics has for its domain persons and societies. It is a kind of value direction, which a moral agent sticks to. It is a property of persons and groups and not of value. In other words, ethos possesses value but value does not possess ethos. This ethos is not an ideal essence like values. It has actual character. To say that ethos has value is to mean that value-essences as principles step into the realm of action. This implies that values do not give themselves up in essentiality and in ideal self-existence. If they were exhausted as the principles of ideal ethical sphere, they would not be ethical principles at all. Our conscience is an example, that is, of values being actual. Otherwise, they would not be ethical principles at all. Values as principles of ethos transcend the realm of ideal self-existence and take possession of the actional sphere, and thus they become the principles of actual ethical sphere. Valuational principles penetrate into the whole sphere of ethical acts and determine them. This determination issues from the values *as principles*. Therefore, this determination of values as principles is the presupposition of the actional sphere. The relation of transcendent ethical acts to the genuine moral values is a conditional relation, since the disposition and will have the power to resist values. The will and disposition can counteract the valuational discernment, which is the *determinant* for moral judgment. That is why they are the "conditions of the possibility" of ethical acts to be valuable.

The specific actuality of values differs from the ideality of values. In the latter, values are supreme determining factors, inviolable and decisive powers; nothing can resist them to be the principle of ideal sphere. But in the former, values are actualized *conditionally*. They are subject to the will and disposition, which may or may not resist them. In actual ethical sphere, they are no longer inviolable determining factor, or absolutely controlling authority. As Hartmann says,

> Here not everything is subordinate to them; the acts of the subject do not accommodate themselves to them unresistingly; they have their own actional laws, determinants of another kind.[56]

Hartmann points out that all moral values have a tendency to be the principles of the ethical sphere of action. That they fail to be so is for lacking the categorical power of determination. If the ethical acts of person are *categorically* determined by values, then their laws must be followed mechanically without exception like a natural process. As a result, values will form a straight-line continuation of existential categories; there would be nothing like actual ethical sphere; nor there will be primal self-existence of values. The antagonism between the transcendent acts of persons and the Idea of right acts, which form the essence of ethical phenomena, will be abolished.

Thirdly, values are also principles of the *real* ethical sphere. We have already pointed out that the specific quality of actuality of values consists in the possibility of conduct to be contrary to values. Even in this disagreement between transcendent act and moral values, the connection between the two is not broken. Rather, it continues in full force. In other words, there is a tension between ontological and axiological principles, which subsists in the same actional sphere. This actional sphere is subordinately called the world of reality. Moral consciousness expresses itself through the actional sphere in transcendent acts. Through the actional sphere, values succeed in moulding the real. It is to be noted here that the real ethical sphere does not consist of only moral agents with his acts; it also includes his living creations, permanent communal customs, etc.

What has been said about the ethical sphere of actions holds equally good for the realm of *real* ethical sphere. Like that of *actual* ethical sphere, values are not decisive determinant power. They are also not fulfilled without resistance in this sphere. Thus, values are, in a restricted sense, the principles of the *real* ethical sphere.

5. Values and their Discovery

We may turn now to another important aspect of Hartmann's value-Platonism, which he deals with at length in chapter, "The

Pathway to the Discovery of Values" in the *Ethics*. Earlier, we have pointed out that values are always "there". They are eternal and immutable having their inherent and dormant power unlike those of fabricated items of the world. We cannot create or modify them. What we can do is to *discover* the already existing values as they are. This discovery of values, according to Hartmann, takes place at two stages: (i) Primary and (ii) Secondary. Let us take one at a time.

1. The discovery that is made at the primary level is what Hartmann calls "the primal sensing of values", which in turn means "a primal, immediate capacity to appreciate the valuable."[57] This is an immediate apprehension of values, a matter of emotional approval or disapproval of something, that is, action or conduct. This sort of discovery is unmediated by concepts, signs, symbols, etc. We shall take up the task of elaborating the nature of this kind of discernment, which is of crucial phenomenological importance, in the chapter titled "Experiencing Values".

2. The second stage of discovery presupposes the first stage mentioned above. That is to say, this sort of discovery takes place only after one has already had the primary discovery of values. This is reflective and intellectual in nature unlike that of primary discovery. This sort of discovery is subordinate to the primary "sensing of values" in the sense that the latter is prior to the former. That is, what is discovered in the primary "sensing" is elevated by reflection and deliberation to a theoretical and systematic level. This is the task of philosophical ethics. Philosophical ethics occupies itself with the analysis of values which others have already discovered. So the principle adopted here is: "one knows it already."[58]

Hartmann is aware of the fact that ethical convictions of mankind and individuals differ and change from time to time and from age to age. But do values also change with the changing ethical convictions? Hartmann's clear response to such a query is that values remain static and unchanged. Values are independent of such changes. For Hartmann, it is not values that change but the *apprehension* of them. Thus, he says,

> In the revolution of the ethos, the values themselves do not shift. Their nature is super-temporal, super-historical. But the consciousness of them shifts.[59]

Values exist in their ideal plane independently of anything whatever be the changes that occur in the goods or persons; values remain as they are. Owing to changes in our apprehension of them "that actions, dispositions, relationships, which yesterday passed as good, can to-day appear bad. Neither the real nor the values have changed."[60]

It is interesting to note as to how the shifting of our value-apprehension takes place. This has been explained in Cadwallader's book, *Searchlight on Values* with the help of an analogy, namely, "searchlight analogy". In this analogy, our value-consciousness is compared with a searchlight and values are conceived of as something existing in a vast field having three-dimensional space, like stars in the sky. Our consciousness, like a searchlight, directs its focus on the ideal plane of values and thereby only a relatively small portion of the vast field of values at a particular point of time or age is "seen". And this implies that a certain ethos-group apprehends those values, which come under the purview of their focus of intuition. Those values that have been under the focus of consciousness may *appear* bad, as with the "wandering about" of the focus of our consciousness, some values are lost on the one hand and some are gained, on the other. Mark here what Hartmann has to say,

> The process of ethical revolution is a genuine process of discovery, a genuine unveiling, a disclosing of values; indeed, on the other side there is always at the same time a loss of values, a forgetting of them, a vanishing. This whole phenomenon of transformation shows a kind of "narrowness" of the valuational consciousness.[61]

To put the matter succinctly, some values lose the attention of consciousness at a particular point of time and some other values come under the focus of valuational consciousness in accordance with the shifting of valuational apprehension. But the point to note here is that values, which get the attention of valuational consciousness, are *not* new values. J.N. Findlay rightly points out,

> Such values are not really new, only hitherto ignored, and they are certainly not the creations of those who suddenly feel them, as Nietzsche thought them to be.[62]

Our valuational consciousness is constantly at work to discover a group of values or other. There is no stopping of each valuational apprehension. But Hartmann maintains that the shifting of value-consciousness does not mean the revaluation of values. If the revaluation of values were possible, then the devaluation of values also would be possible, which would make values something manufactured and thereby they would be subjective. The shifting of value-apprehension brings about the revaluation of *life*. People or individuals of a certain culture or ethos-group revalue their life by having discovered a set of values, and thereby stimulating their life and giving it a new significance and direction.

Notes

1. This has widely been acknowledged. Please see,
   (1) J.N. Mohanty, *Nicolai Hartmann and Alfred North Whitehead*, (Progressive Publishers, Calcutta, 1957).
   (2) E.H. Cadwallader, *Searchlight on Values*, (University Press of America, Lanham, 1984).
   (3) F. Kraenzel, "Nicolai Hartmann's Doctrine of Ideal Values: An Examination." *The Journal of Value Inquiry*, Vol. 18, No. 2, 1984.
2. Hartmann, N. *Ethics*, op. cit. p. 184.
3. Cadwallader, E.H. *Searchlight on Values*, op. cit. p. 3.
4. Ibid., p. 185.
5. Kraenzel, F. "Nicolai Hartmann's Doctrine of Ideal Values: An Examination," *The Journal of Value Inquiry*, Vol. 18, No. 2, 1984, p. 300.
6. Hartmann, N. *Ethics*, op. cit. p. 62, (our emphasis).
7. Ibid., p. 98.
8. Ibid., p. 185.
9. Ibid.
10. Ibid.
11. Ibid., p. 225.
12. Ibid., p. 218.

13. Ibid.
14. Ibid., p. 217.
15. Ibid., p. 218.
16. Ibid.
17. Ibid., p. 219.
18. Ibid., p. 185.
19. Ibid., p. 177.
20. Ibid., p. 88.
21. Ibid., p. 219.
22. Ibid., p. 220.
23. Ibid., p. 221, (our emphasis).
24. Ibid.
25. Ibid., p. 303, (our emphases).
26. Ibid., p. 221.
27. Mohanty, J.N. *Nicolai Hartmann and Alfred North Whitehead*, (Progressive Publishers, Calcutta, 1957), p. 7.
28. Hartmann, N. *Ethics,* op. cit. p. 193. I acknowledge here that in making clear Hartmann's sense of *a priori*, I have followed Cadwallader's interpretation.
29. Ibid., p. 192.
30. Ibid., p. 193.
31. Cadwallader, E.H. *Searchlight on Values*, op. cit. p. 115.
32. Hartmann, N. *Ethics*, op. cit. p. 186.
33. Ibid., p. 217.
34. Ibid., p. 186.
35. Ibid., p. 192.
36. Ibid., pp. 186-187.
37. Ibid., p. 189. (our emphases)
38. Ibid.
39. Ibid., p. 186.
40. Ibid., p. 187.
41. Ibid.
42. Ibid., p. 192.
43. Ibid., p. 193. (our emphases)
44. Ibid., p. 196.
45. Ibid., p. 185.
46. Ibid., p. 207.
47. Ibid., p. 189.

48. Ibid., p. 208.
49. Ibid., p. 210.
50. Ibid., p. 211.
51. Ibid., p. 213.
52. Ibid., p. 214.
53. Ibid., p. 235.
54. Ibid.
55. Ibid.
56. Ibid., p. 237.
57. Ibid., p. 86.
58. Ibid., p. 93.
59. Ibid., p. 88.
60. Ibid., p. 89.
61. Ibid.
62. Findlay, J.N. *Axiological Ethics*, (Macmillan and Co. Ltd., London, 1970), pp. 74-75.

6

Scheler's Value-Ethics

Scheler's edifice of value-ethics provides an in-depth study of the nature and apprehension of values based as it is on Husserl's phenomenological framework. He openly expresses his indebtedness "to the significant works of Edmund Husserl the methodological consciousness of the unity and sense of the phenomenological attitude ..."[1] and makes use of phenomenological tools, of course in his own manner, to understand the general logic of value-discourse. Another interesting feature of Scheler's ethical thought in *Formalism in Ethics and Non-Formal Ethics of Values,* is his constant reference to Kant and his ethical ideas. His objective of taking into consideration Kant's ethical views is mainly to *refute* formal apriorism in ethics *as such,* of which Kant's ethics serves as an example, and also to refute some specific doctrines of the *Critique of Practical Reason* and thereby to set free German moral thought from Kantian rigorism and imperativism. Moreover, in order to strengthen his position, Scheler also takes a critical look at some traditional ethical doctrines such as, eudaemonism, utilitarianism, and pragmatic-positivistic ethics. Let us first discuss Scheler's understanding of phenomenological method before taking up an exposition of the nature of values.

I. Scheler's Conception of Phenomenology

Scheler is said to be a value-theorist belonging to phenomenological tradition. But his interpretation of the nature of phenomenological techniques has its own uniqueness (of which he is quite conscious). Scheler is decisively influenced mainly by

Husserl's earlier thoughts. He acknowledges the importance of Husserl's *Logical Investigations,* while he remains critical of Husserl's some other works, like *Ideas I* for its egological Cartesianism. He rejects the pre-eminence of logico-theoretical reason given to it by Husserl and insists on the primacy of emotional mode of cognition.

Generally speaking, while Husserl is seen to be concerned with the foundational issues of the nature of phenomenology, Scheler is mainly concerned with applying phenomenology to the field of values. Husserl shares Descartes' concern to establish philosophy on a firm ground, which is able to provide certainty in the realm of knowledge. He is preoccupied with discovering a procedure of "*thinking about*" facts. That is, Husserl's primary concern is to discover a method of philosophical analysis. So he talks of transcendental ego or the ontological question of Being. But to Scheler, unlike Husserl, the question of method is secondary. Instead of the phenomenological investigation of transcendental ego or the ontological question of Being, the focal point of Scheler's interest is the *Being* of Man in his different dimensions, and in the *Formalism in Ethics,* his focus is turned mainly on the valuational aspect of man. It needs to be stressed here that Scheler takes phenomenology not as a philosophical method, but as an *attitude* of inner vision to discover the genealogy of values and emotions. For Scheler, it is basically a procedure of *seeing.* As Scheler writes,

> In the first place, phenomenology is neither the name of a new science nor a substitute for the word "philosophy"; it is the name of an attitude of spiritual seeing in which one can see [*er-schauen*] or experience [*er-leben*] something which otherwise remains hidden, namely, a realm of facts of a particular kind. I say "attitude," not "method."[2]

Thus our two philosophers differ in their respective concerns, and consequently on the procedural question. To our understanding, Scheler seems to be guided by Husserl's theory of intentionality, the doctrine of phenomenological reduction, phenomenological intuition and the doctrine of ideal objects without *always* adhering to the original meaning given to them by Husserl. Having received an unorthodox interpretation in the hands of

Scheler, these distinctive phenomenological features become qualified and further suitable for exploring the realm of values and emotions. He also adheres to the central ideal of phenomenology to be presuppositionless in order to come into immediate contact with the "things" themselves, that is, the essences themselves. Now, we shall concern ourselves with Schelerian version of phenomenology with a view to getting at the heart of his theory of values.

To begin with, what we are to understand by phenomenological or "pure" facts *a la* Scheler, as distinguished from the natural fact on the one hand and the scientific facts, on the other. Natural facts refer to the world of our common sense experience of the natural attitude in its different dimensions. These are the facts of natural world where we live and carry our daily business out and we take it for granted that the world of concrete things and events will remain as it is whether we perceive it or not. But the scientific facts are *artificial* unlike the natural facts, in the sense that science does not create or make things and events of the world the object of *direct* inspection but "constructs" all these through what Scheler calls "scientific reduction". Like natural facts, scientific facts are also concerned with concrete things and events but in a *symbolic* and *artificial* manner. These facts are understood, not in terms of tradition, but in terms of generalization, idealization, etc.

In Scheler's view, phenomenological facts are quite different from both natural and scientific facts in that the former are independent of all sensory factors but the latter are *not*. To quote Scheler,

> The phenomenological fact is a *pure* fact, that is, one from which all possible elements of sensation have been eliminated. Phenomenological seeing is "intuition" or pure intuition, in which the sensory functions no longer play a (intentional) role.[3]

The pure fact which is "given" as a content of immediate intuition always remains as an "intuitive identity" in spite of the changes that occur in sensory functions. That is, this kind of fact maintains the character of an independent variable unlike that of sensory content (natural or scientific) which is a dependent variable. The sensory content is dependent on pure fact for its foundation and not *vice versa*. Further, what Scheler calls "intuitive identity" of pure fact can *never* be symbolic. That is to say, the pure fact cannot be designated by any possible pictures, symbols, signs, etc. like that of natural or scientific fact. As Scheler explains,

> Phenomenological experience in this sense furnishes the facts themselves and does so directly, that is, without symbols or signs, in contrast to any nonphenomenological experience, for example, natural intuition, or scientific experience. Phenomenological experience is asymbolic experience. The phenomenological fact is, in the first place, an asymbolic fact.[4]

On Scheler's theory, the phenomenological facts or "pure" facts are *a priori* in a peculiar and novel sense, and not *a posteriori,* the latter being the case of natural and scientific facts. Now, the question is: what is meant by "a priori" here?

> We designate as "*a priori*" all those ideal units of meaning and those propositions that are self-given by way of an *immediate intuitive* content in the absence of any kind of positing [*Setzung*] of subjects that think them and of the real nature of those subjects, and in the absence of any kind of positing of objects to which such units of meaning are applicable.[5]

Thus "a priori", for Scheler, means *ideal* units of meaning or signification which neither posits the existence of a subject who would think them, nor the existence of an object to which such units of signification can be applied. Apriority here means "self-givenness" and is discovered by the knowing subject in *eidetic* intuition. Scheler cites the example of a case of deception. Suppose that one takes something to be alive, though it is not so; here, essence or "whatness" of life is intuitively given in case of deception. Obviously, this "whatness" or "fact" does not have ontological status and hence, it is *pure a priori* as a datum of eidetic intuition. "The point, therefore, is to leave aside all kinds of *positing,* including the positing of 'real' or 'non-real,' 'illusion' or 'real,' etc."[6] Now this intuitive content can be called "phenomenon", though this is not to be confused with "appearance", supposedly behind which something is assumed to be hidden. The word "phenomenon" here has been taken in the Husserlian sense so as to mean something which *wholly shows itself*. Nothing lies behind it. That is, essence or phenomenon means absolute showing of what is given to intuitive insight. This is the *a priori* essence or "whatness" of an object, which is known through phenomenological intuition or what Scheler calls, "essential intuiting". It is to be noted here that there is no question of degree in such "givenness" of a phenomenon. "Either this 'what' is intuited and, hence, 'self'-given (totally and without subtraction, neither by way of a 'picture' nor by way of a 'symbol'), or this 'what' is *not* intuited and, hence, not given."[7]

At this stage, a few misgivings regarding *"a priori"* must be removed. The *a priori*, which Scheler talks of, is not conceptual *a priori* as Kant conceives. Scheler rejects Kant's transcendental sense of "a priori", which is formal and conceptual. What Scheler calls "pure fact" is an "a priori" and it cannot be grasped by any formal concept but by "essential intuiting". Secondly, in the Kantian sense, the sensible manifolds have to "conform" to the *a priori* laws in order to be a piece of knowledge. But the "conforming," in Scheler's sense, means that real things and acts are to "conform" to *a priori* content or values in order to be valuable. So the *a priori* in the latter sense is not be confused with the Copernican turn to which Kant draws our attention. Thirdly, Scheler points out that the apriority of "facts" has nothing to do with the dichotomy of "innate" and "acquired" ideas of the Cartesian mode which are causal and genetic and not applicable to the type of insight with which we are concerned here.

Like Husserl, Scheler also favours distinguishing essences or what he calls "pure facts" on one hand and concepts/propositions, on the other. On Scheler's view, "pure facts" are positive data of phenomenological experience but the concepts are bearers of all inductive knowledge. Further, pure facts are not linguistic units. But the concepts are linguistic units and in a sense symbolic. Moreover, pure facts are registered and reported as "given". The concepts, on the other hand, are symbolic and work as part of judgments. So Scheler writes,

> The concept "thing" and the intuited "thingness", the concept equality and the intuited equality, or the being-equal (as distinguished from the being-similar), etc., must be clearly distinguished.[8]

These distinctions imply that Scheler would not confound "intuitive content" with "concept" in ethical domain in keeping with the spirit of phenomenological method. For Scheler, the process of "eidetic" cognition is totally non-conceptual, while the process of thought is carried out through concepts.

According to Scheler, all concepts and propositions find their fulfillment in *such* pure facts. They must conform to such facts in order to be true prior to all sensory experience as well as induction. And this *truth* of concepts and propositions is *totally* independent of the entire domain of sensory and inductive experience; and therefore, *this* cannot be cancelled or refuted by such experience. These pure facts are dependent neither on propositions, nor on the acts of judgement, which corresponds them. Rather, all propositions including those of positive sciences are dependent on these "facts" in order to find their fulfillment in the latter to be true. "Hence," Scheler says, "we expressly reject any given *a priori* 'concept' or 'proposition' that does not permit complete fulfillment by a *fact* of intuition."[9] In positive terms, he writes,

> ... the a priori belongs wholly to the *"given"* and the sphere of *facts.* A proposition is only a priori true (or false) insofar as it finds its fulfillment in *such* "facts."[10]

The one point that merits attention here is that the *a priori* "facts" that are "given" to pure intuition are not amenable to observation and verification. They can neither be suspended nor cancelled by observation nor by induction, nor can they be further improved. Rather, *they* give the empirical observation and induction the desired direction. It is the essential nature of a "given content" that it cannot be observed but is always *intuited.* It is the criterion of such *a priori* facts having interconnection among them that they are *always* presupposed. The only way to make them "seen" is by pointing to them.

Scheler adopts Husserl's dictum that "consciousness is always consciousness of something," that is, the knowing consciousness is *intentional* in character. It is only the intentional acts of consciousness, which grasps all things, events, and values as *meant* object. This is what is called phenomenological intuition or experience. There may be different forms of intentional acts, such as, acts of feeling, of loving and hating, which reveal the "pure facts" that are otherwise hidden.

We may distinguish phenomenological experience from sensory-experience as Scheler does in order to further characterize the former in terms of the following *two* criteria:

1. In phenomenological experience, "pure facts" themselves are "given". This is made possible without recourse to any mediated means such as symbols, signs, or instructions. One may define, for example, the colour blue in different ways, as the colour of this or that object extensively, as the colour designated by the word "blue," as the colour I am now seeing, etc. But in all these ways of defining the essence "blue" is common. It is the basic pure fact, which is *essentially* and *in itself* given. It is in such "experience" *alone* that the "fact" blue "in person" is given and not in the experience of sensory nature. It is the pure fact of intuition as distinguished from natural and scientific fact, which is "given" *immediately* and *directly.* No presupposition or mediation of concepts, propositions, symbols, signs, etc. are required to have an intuitive insight into the *facts themselves.* Rather, in phenomenological experience "the totality of these signs, instructions, and kinds of determination find their *basic* fulfilment."[11]

2. The second criterion for distinguishing phenomenological experience from inductive experience is that the former is *immanent act* and never anything outside of such act can belong or given to it. But in the case of ordinary experience, its object is always *transcendent* to the act of experiencing. And that which is not given in the act of experiencing is "meant". In the case of our experiencing a chair, for example, the chair itself as spatio-temporal object does not belong to the act of experiencing a chair. Phenomenological experience is different. In Scheler's words,

> ... phenomenological experience is an *immanent* experience; that is, only that which can itself be intuited in an act right now belongs to it, in contrast to every "transcending", nonphenomenological experience, in which something is

> "meant" or "supposed" [*vermeint*] which is not intuitively given in it.[12]

In phenomenological experience, what is intuitively given in the intentional act is never something, which belongs outside of the domain of such acts. The intuitive content belongs to the immanent sphere of intentional acts. In short, in phenomenological experience, the intentional act and its object as "meant" are not separated off. That is, in phenomenological experience, the intentional acts are directed towards its *own* kind of object as "meant" both of which belong to the *same* immanent domain. In other words, "what is intended or meant" and "what is given" are no two different domains. The congruence of what is "*intended*" with what is "*given*" gives rise to phenomenological experience. To quote Scheler,

> In phenomenological experience nothing is *meant* that is not *given,* and nothing is given that is not meant. It is precisely *in* this *coincidence* of the "meant" and the "given" that the *content* of phenomenological experience alone becomes *manifest* [Kundwerden]. *In* this coincidence, in the very meeting *point* of fulfillment of what is meant and what is given, the phenomenon *appears.*[13]

Summarily, Scheler has taken his methodological principles over from Husserl's phenomenology and interprets them in his own way to turn them efficient instruments in order to discover the realm of values and emotions. In our view, Scheler remains true to the phenomenological ideal of a presuppositionless philosophy when he appeals to his reader to disregard the *thatness* of things and look for *whatness* of things. He adopts Husserl's slogan "Back to things themselves", and in keeping with the phenomenological spirit, he describes values as "phenomena", and *not* as concepts. For him, it is intentionality of the knowing consciousness, or what he calls "feeling-acts", which enables one aprioricically to discover the value-phenomena or value-facts – the data of moral consciousness. This intentionality of feeling-acts has been described by Scheler as "goal-determined movement". The intentional movement of feeling-acts enables one to apprehend the "objects", i.e., values. Like Husserl, Scheler describes phenomenological experience as *immanent, direct* and *immediate* experience. In ethics, Scheler adopts the emotional mode of cognition as a suitable means of apprehending values. Above all, Scheler's objective of adopting phenomenological methodology in his value-ethics is to discover the invariant and essential structures of valuational aspect of *man,* the centre of all philosophizing.

II. Scheler's Non-formal Value-ethics

As an anti-thesis to the ethical system of Kant, Scheler develops his own ethical theory founding it on the aforesaid basic ideas from Husserlian phenomenology. As against Kantian formal ethics, Scheler builds up a *non*-formal theory of value. Regarding his value-theory, he says:

> The spirit behind my ethics is one of rigid ethical absolutism and objectivism. My position may in another respect be called "emotional intuitionism" and "non-formal apriorism."[14]

Scheler finally interprets his philosophical position in his value-ethics as "ethical personalism" which he puts as the subtitle of his main work. He believes that all values, i.e., the values of things and beings, are subordinated to values of the *person.*

1. Values as Distinguished from their Bearers

Scheler's ethical work opens with distinguishing things, goods, and values. Goods are defined as "*things* of value", i.e., as things in which values are realized, and values are what belong to things, i.e., "thing-values". Values are essentially independent of goods which are their bearers in respect of their being and givenness. In order to demonstrate the fact that the being of values is independent of things, state of affairs, men and relation of all kinds which are their bearers, Scheler puts forward the following reasons. First, in order to distinguish values from their bearers, Scheler refers to the analogy that values share with colour. We perceive a colour, say, red in different surfaces of empirical things, for example, on blood, flag, etc. But the colour "red" itself is totally independent of these things on the surface of which it appears. For it is possible to talk of "red" as a pure colour without experiencing the need to conceive of it as covering a surface.

Similarly, though a value is found attached to natural objects, it is not dependent on its natural bearers. For, it is possible to talk about such values as "agreeable," "charming," "friendly" and the like, without conceiving of them as qualities belonging to any thing or person. In Scheler's words,

> Just as I can bring to givenness a red color as a mere extensive quale, e.g., as a pure color of the spectrum, without regarding it as covering a corporeal surface or as something spatial, so also are such *values* as agreeable, charming, lovely, friendly, distinguished, and noble in principle accessible to me without my having to represent them as properties belonging to things or men.[15]

In a word, in Scheler's view, values are distinct from their bearers in which they are assumed to be instantiated. Secondly, values are distinct from our subjective emotional states, which are also their bearers. One may feel sad for his friend's sudden death and this may evoke in his mind certain subjective feeling-states. He may feel calm, heartbroken, or hostile in attitude etc. And these subjective psychological states vary and change rapidly, but the feeling of sadness subsists invariantly. *This* clearly demonstrates that "... feeling-states of all kinds neither are nor condition values; they can at best be *bearers* of values."[16] Further, what evokes a disposition or a state of feeling in someone's mind is quite different from its meant object. That is, the cause of a feeling-state like heartbrokenness or defiance is not identical with the object, which is intended and meant. Thirdly, that values "exist" and are given clearly and evidentially *apart from* their bearers can be made clear from the cases of our daily experiences. In the case of a person who may strike us as pleasant or repugnant without being able to say *why* this is the case. Or we may consider a work of art as something beautiful or ugly, distinguished or commonplace without our being able to indicate which properties of the work make it so. This is equally true of all psycho-physical existents. "Clearly", Scheler writes,

> neither the experience of values nor the degree of the adequation and the evidence (adequation in a full sense plus

> evidence constitutes the "self-givenness" of a value) depends in any way on the experience of the bearer of the values.[17]

Fourthly, Scheler further points out that the *meaning* of a thing or a relation, (that is, what a thing or a relation is) may change in different contexts in which it is used *without* having any variance in its value. *This* also implies that values are, in their being, *independent* of their bearers. Fifthly, to distinguish a value from its object/state-of-affairs to which it is attached, we do not require the pre-given knowledge of its bearer/state-of-affairs. Scheler cites the example of wine. According to him, to distinguish the *value* of wine from its bearers, it is *not* at all necessary to have the pre-given knowledge of its bearers, that is, the knowledge of its ingredients and the methods of its preparation. For a value-complex is not mere value *of* state-of-affairs. In fact, a value is *not* "given" under the condition in which we grasp a state-of-affair. "Indeed", Scheler concludes,

> it is as if the *axiological nuance* of an object (whether it be remembered, anticipated, represented, or perceived) were the *first* factor that came upon us, ... A value precedes its object, it is the first "messenger" of its particular nature. An object may be vague and unclear while its value is already distinct and clear.[18]

Scheler's point is that the value of certain object precedes its bearer; we do not extract a value from a valuable object. Rather, a value is prior to them. The realization of a value in it as a real presence in it confers upon it the particular value. Sixthly, that values are different from their bearers is also clear from the fact that values themselves do not change with the changes that occur in their bearers. Just as colour "blue" does not become red when a blue sphere becomes red, so the *value* of friendship remains unchanged even if a friend of mine turns against me and betrays. Seventhly, value-qualities are different from what human beings value or consider important. For example, a painting by M.F. Hussain is beautiful, *not* because what people think according to social validity but because the beauty is found *in* the painting independently of people's opinion. Values, according to Scheler, are objective "facts" of morality or aesthetics. Lastly, in their mode of givenness also, according to Scheler, values are different from their bearers. Values are given in and through *im*mediate means of intentional feeling-acts while their bearers are given through the *mediated* means of sensuous intuition. Scheler, therefore, distinguishes *goods* or what he calls *"value-things"* from mere values which he designates as *"thing-values"*.

2. Values as *a priori* "facts" of Morality

To begin with, values, according to Scheler, are "pure facts" or what he calls "value-facts." In ethical sphere, they are "moral facts" or moral value-facts, or what Scheler calls *"independent facts of the moral life."*[19] To recall our characterization of phenomenological facts or pure facts made earlier, value-facts are independent of all sensory characters. All possible sensory factors are eliminated from these value-facts and therefore, they are stripped of all transcendences. Further, for Scheler, values are what belong to a specific mode of experience. That is, they are available to us as pure intuitive contents in immediate "experience", and *not* in sense-experience like those of natural facts. In ethical sphere, according to Scheler,

> Moral facts, as opposed to the sphere of meanings, are *facts of non-formal intuition, not* of sensible intuition, if by "intuition" we mean immediacy of the givenness of an object and not necessarily a picture-like content.[20]

Furthermore, value-facts, being in the nature of "pure facts", (the nature of which we have discussed earlier) maintain a kind of "intuitive identity," and remain as independent variable despite the changes that occur in the persons, in his acts and in his psychological states of mind, which are their carriers, the latter being the dependent variables. The idea that values remain fixed while person's feeling-states may change has been expressed by Scheler in the following passage:

> The *value* can also remain constant before our eyes while our feeling-state and its expressions undergo manifold changes. A thousand different feeling-states – joy, anger, ire, pride, or feelings of being offended – may fleet by us while facing a

> person whom we value and hold in high esteem, but without the involvement of our value-consciousness – let alone the value itself. Such states are tied not to certain values but to concrete situations, to which our *bodily* thereness always belongs, too.[21]

Moreover, an object, or an act of person, is dependent on these "autonomous *value-facts*"[22] of morality in order to be something of value. In other words, a good or an act always has its foundation in the comprehension of value-contents lying in the object or act. Therefore, it is on these moral facts that the whole of ethics stands, and with them it falls. But it must be noted that the word "fact" here has been used in a technical sense to signify the being of values as independent, autonomous and "fixed" being.

In continuation of his characterizations of value-facts, Scheler says that values are "de-symbolizing phenomena" which has nothing do with "appearances" in Kantian sense. Here, again, we may recall the distinction we have made earlier between concepts and *pure* facts. Value-facts are autonomous "*facts,*" and not concepts. What are meant by concepts, according to Scheler, are *symbols* that are used for representing values. In Scheler's words,

> The names used for moral values in propositions which predicate them as *properties* of certain volitional acts, deeds, or persons – e.g., "good," "evil," "noble," "base" – are therefore only *symbols* for the quality and the degree of *success* which, under average circumstances in a given volitional sphere, an act of will and a deed will have after such approval or disapproval. Hence *no* specific *factual state of affairs* corresponds to these names.[23]

Husserl's distinction between concepts and essences has been accepted by Scheler, and accordingly, he makes a distinction between value-*concept* and value-*content.* The value-judgements have to "agree" or "conform" to these value-facts or essences in order to be objective and meaningful expressions. In other words, value-judgements always have to "mean" or "signify" these value-facts in order to find fulfillment in them, and thereby to be *a priori* true. Thus, according to Scheler,

> Every value-statement is directed toward a content that is capable and needy of adequate intuitional cognition.[24]

For Scheler, it is only the intuition of a phenomenological kind that is capable of grasping the "value-phenomena" themselves without any mediation of concepts, symbols, signs, or instructions. For, he is quite aware of the fact that the danger of symbolism lay in the tendency of symbols to displace and to conceal the "phenomena". So Scheler clearly states that

> ... values are not concepts abstracted from empirical, concrete things, men, or deeds; nor are they abstract, "dependent" moments of such things. They are *independent phenomena* that are comprehended independent of the peculiarity of contents, as well as of the being-real or the being-ideal and the non-being (in this twofold sense) of their bearers.[25]

Now, our characterization of value-facts as distinguished from concepts, symbols, etc. paves the way for us to understand in *what* sense values are *a priori* facts. Scheler takes values to be *a priori* in a new and peculiar sense. In keeping with the meaning of his definition of *a priori*, which we have explained in the context of elaborating his conception of phenomenology, Scheler identifies values with the "intuitive content" as given in pure immediate intuition. Values as *a priori* facts refer to "ideal units" of signification, which neither posits the existence of a person who "bears" them, nor posits any object to which they are applicable. Scheler's concept of apriority of values does not implicate any kind of positing. According to Scheler,

> ... it is indeed possible to find a non-formal series of values, with its order, which is *totally* independent of the world of goods and its changing forms, and which is *a priori* to such a world of goods.[26]

Elsewhere he says, "A value precedes its object, it is the first 'messenger' of its particular nature."[27] It follows now that values, as *a priori* facts, which are of ideal nature, are "found" in immediate intuition as its content. This is distinguishable from Kant's "forms of understanding", as also from the natural or scientific facts. Obviously, Scheler's concept of *a priori* signifies concrete "facts" of morality. He is struggling for values as "material a priori" instead of "formal a priori" in the Kantian sense.

3. Values as Ideal Objects

According to Scheler, values are objects. In his own words, "As value-phenomena (no matter if in the order of appearance or reality), values are *true objects* and are different from all *states* of feeling."[28] Elsewhere, he says that values are "*genuinely* objective objects."[29] Now, what does it mean to say that values are "*objects*"? This question may be answered as in the following: (i) Values are objects, in the sense that they are given to *pure immediate intuition* and are distinguishable from mere concepts. Unlike natural facts which are objects of sense-experience, value-facts are objects of non-formal intuitive act of phenomenological kind. "The value itself," Scheler holds, "always must be *intuitively given* or must refer back to that kind of givenness."[30] Here, objecthood of values, in our view, is *epistemological.* (ii) The view that values are objects also means that they are not derived from our experience of the persons, acts, or things. They are also not concepts abstracted from the persons, acts or things. Rather, values are independent of all these things and their changing forms. They have their autonomy and independence. In Scheler's words, they are "independent and qualitatively differentiated moral value-facts."[31] Elsewhere, he terms them as "autonomous facts". Thus the being of values has their own unique mode of existence that is not at all dependent on anything else. They are eternal, immutable, and self-contained being. In short, the peculiar and differentiated mode of givenness and the alleged autonomy and independence from everything else are, in our view, what constitute the objecthood of values.

Now, for Scheler, these objects (i.e., values) are not real in the manner of chairs and tables. For, values do not exist in space and time. Nor are they fictitious or imaginary. They also cannot be wished away. For, they exist genuinely. The question is: What is their mode of existence? For Scheler, values are *ideal* objects. In his own words, "Value-qualities, however, are "*ideal objects,*" as are qualities of colors and sounds."[32] Scheler compares the status of the being of values with colour to mean that values exist *the way* species colour as distinguished from the individual shade of colour exists, and the values are given *the way* the colour species are intuited. It is true that an individual shade of a colour is temporal and is given to our sense-perception. But the colour spectrum is *not* temporal, and is given not to sense-perception but to a pure intuition. This means that a colour spectrum, unlike an individual shade of a colour, is *ideal*. It is in *this* precise sense of the term "ideal" that the values are *ideal* objects. We may note here that Scheler has taken over *this* meaning of "ideal" from Husserl, which we shall have occasion to critically discuss later.

Scheler's objective of comparing values with colour spectrum is, therefore, to show that just as a colour spectrum has non-spatio-temporal existence and is intuited through a non-sensuous means, values have non-spatio-temporal existence, and are grasped through a direct intuition. The categories of space and time are not applicable to colour-spectrum and values alike. Both are not posited by us but are disclosed in what Husserl calls "categorial intuition". All these mean that values, like colour spectrum, as distinguished from individual shade of colour are *ideal* in nature. The crux of the matter is that values as *ideal* objects are neither spatio-temporal, nor fictitious or non-sensical but something that exist as, to repeat Scheler's own phrase, "*genuinely* objective objects". To say that values are ideal objects does not, however, mean that they do not have any contact with the existing order of things. Scheler explains this point in the following passage:

> It is only in goods that values become "real." They are not yet real in valuable things. In a good, however, a value is *objective* (whatever the value may be) *and real* at the same time. There is a *genuine* increase of value in the real world with any new good.[33]

Implicit herein is the idea that values are given *in* this world, in the sense that they are intuited in goods and persons. Though the values are essentially ideal in nature, they are objectified and become real in the world of goods and persons only, which "represents a 'thinglike' unity of value-qualities or value-complexes which is founded in a specific basic value."[34] But this does not mean that values are dependent on goods in which they are apprehended. On the contrary, values are independent of man and goods, yet can only be intuited in them. In other words, it is only through directing our gaze to specific goods or men that it is possible to "intend" or "mean" a value in intuition, even though the realm of values is independent of the world of goods and of man.

Hence, it is obvious that Scheler rejects the Platonic sense of "ideal" to describe the nature of values. For him, values are not ideal in the sense Plato conceives of Ideas as ideal entities. Instead, he accords to values the "existence" like a species colour as distinguished from individual shade of colour. Further, unlike Plato's Ideas, values, for Scheler, are resident of *this* world, in the sense that they are caught in eidetic intuition only *in* goods and persons. Finally, values are not also real as Platonic Ideas are having an existence in a non-spatio-temporal world. Rather, they *become* real and elements of the natural world in a good, though they are essentially ideal. Therefore, Scheler says,

> In fact, I reject, in principle and at the very *threshold* of philosophy, a heavenly realm of ideas and values that is "independent" of the essence and *execution* of living spiritual *acts,* independent not *only* with regard to man and human consciousness but also with regard to the *essence and execution of a living spirit in general.*[35]

4. Values as Given to Feeling-acts

On Scheler's view, "Values are given first of all in *feeling* [Fuehlen]."[36] Values are given to us as intentional objects of feeling just as colour species are intuited in and through non-sensible intuition. Our faculty of reason is not the *right* means of getting access to the realm of values as the latter are beyond the grasp of intellect. So Scheler recognizes that

> … there is a type of experiencing whose "objects" are completely inaccessible to reason; reason is as blind to them as ears and hearing are blind to colors. It is a kind of experience that leads us to *genuinely* objective objects and the eternal order among them, i.e., to *values* and the order of ranks among them. And the order and laws contained in this experience are as exact and evident as those of logic and mathematics;[37]

Scheler thus discovers in the existential man a cognitive phase in emotional life which enables him to grasp values. And this phase is in no way inferior to that of intellect in respect of cognitive capability.

Scheler is quite aware that a dichotomy between reason and emotion has been maintained throughout the passage of the history of philosophy, and emotion is always given comparatively a lower value than reason or intellect. Emotional life of man has been regarded as a world of complete chaos and therefore, it cannot be a guide to our moral choices, i.e., what ought to be done or ought not to be done. As a consequence, Scheler points out,

> ... ethics has in the course of its history been constituted either as absolute and a priori, and therefore rational, or as relative, empirical, and emotional. That ethics can and must be both absolute *and* emotional has rarely even been considered.[38]

Needless to mention, it is Scheler, therefore, who makes a decisive attempt to lay the foundation of an ethics which is "both absolute *and* emotional" at the same time. Keeping himself in line with Blaise Pascal, he elaborates a "correct" theory of the sort of feeling that is concerned with value-experience. Scheler explains the nature of feeling-*acts* through which values are given by distinguishing them from mere feeling-*states*. In the first place, emotional acts or what we have called feeling-acts, according to Scheler, are *"feeling of something."*[39] This means that the feeling-acts are intentional in character and that their intentionality is directed towards some "objects", that is, *values*. So there is a kind of intentional relatedness between feeling-acts and their objects which is *un*mediated by anything else. On the contrary, feeling-states are purely psychological states of mind, which may or may not have objects. If there is any object, the feeling-states are "related" to the former by way of objectifying acts, such as, of sensation, perception, thinking or representation. For example, a psychological state of mind, say, sadness occurs in me due to my failure in the examination. Here I "relate" my psychological state of sadness to my failure in examination through objectifying act of "thinking". So, *this* kind of relatedness is always *mediate.* Secondly, feeling-states are not *of themselves* related to their objects. They do *not* go *directly* over to their objects, if there happens to be any object at all. There is no "immanent directedness" towards any object. But the feeling-acts are *of themselves* related to their objects. The intentionality of feeling-acts goes *directly* over to their objects, i.e., *values.* "For here we do not feel 'about something; we immediately feel *something,* i.e., a specific value-quality."[40] The immanently directed intentionality reaches its objects directly and immediately, i.e., values. Thirdly, a feeling-state is related only to what is outside of it or transcendent to consciousness. Such relatedness, according to Scheler, is *not* "original". On the contrary, the relatedness between feeling-act and its object subsists in an immanent realm and is therefore "original". In Scheler's words, "feeling (i.e., feeling-acts) *originally* intends its *own* kind of objects, namely, *'values'.*"[41] Finally, feeling-states are dead and factual states of mind. "There is no 'signifying' in it, nor is there any immanent directness in it."[42] But, on the contrary, feeling-acts have signification that is "capable of fulfillment" and "non-fulfillment."[43] Feeling-acts are signifying acts in the sense that they are capable of providing us with the knowledge of values, unlike those of feeling-states which are merely dead state of mind. In other words, intentionality of feeling-acts is what Scheler calls "goal-determined movement."[44] That is, it is a movement of emotional intentionality to bring some meaning into the focus of knowing consciousness to grasp a thing or an action in its value-aspect. This intentional feeling-act, unlike psychological states of mind, presents to us some mundane object or action of a person with some spiritual meaning, that is, values.

There is now the question: how are values given to such feeling-acts? In Scheler's view, values are given to such feeling-acts when we encounter goods and persons. The intended objects of feeling-acts are values which is given *originally* and *immediately* without recourse to the objectifying acts of representing, judging, etc. The originality and immediacy of givenness of values in essential intuition mean that they are given with utmost clarity and evidence. Just as an individual shade of colour is given to our sensible intuition, so are the values given in our essential intuition through cognitive intentional feeling-acts. At this stage, it appears that Scheler believes that there must be an object to the intentionality of feeling-acts. Notice what he says to characterize the intentionality of feeling-acts. He says,

> ... we understand *intentional* to indicate only those experiences that can *mean* an object and in whose execution an objective content can *appear*. This occurs only in emotional experiences, which, in a strict sense, constitute value-feeling.[45]

Elsewhere, he says, "to knowledge (and indeed all intentional acts) a being must correspond ... ."[46] These statements of Scheler are purported to mean that there must be an "*existent*" object, i.e., a value corresponding to each intentional feeling-act. In other words, the intentionality of feeling-act cannot be directed towards *no* kind of existent being.

We have mentioned earlier that Scheler appeals to the analogy that values share with colour to illustrate the manner in which values exist and given to our immediate intuition. Scheler's use of this analogy is said to have been inspired by Husserl's theory of universals as it is found in latter's *Investigation II*, namely, "The Ideal Unity of the Species and Modern Theories of Abstraction."[47] Scheler seems to have substantiated the following three points in the main with reference to Husserl's theory of Universals:

(a) Just as an individual shade of red requires a surface for its appearance, so also values require substrates for them to exist, while both individual shade of red and values remain independent of what they appear on. (b) One can talk of a pure colour of the spectrum without need to conceive of it as covering a surface. Similarly, values can be a content of immediate intuition without their instantiation in any empirical object. Though we perceive goods through our senses but our intuitive gaze is directed toward values to have the apprehension of them. (c) Scheler regards values as *ideal objects* in the same way for Husserl species colour is an ideal object given through an intuitive act.

4. Values as Relative to their Comprehension

Let us turn to an important and peculiar feature of Scheler's value-ethics, namely, the relativity of the comprehension of values. It is a historical fact of some importance that imperatives and norms change from one social group to another or one race to another. For that matter, the different social groups practice diverse ethics or the same society upholds some values at the present time, which may differ markedly from what they were in earlier times. Thus different social groups or successive generations within the same society may have different norms and imperatives for the evaluation of conduct. Now, the question is: how is the fact of the divergence of norms in different societies or generations compatible with the thesis that the values are eternal and absolute? Do values too vary with the changes that occur in norms followed by different societies?

Scheler argues that having different norms in historically existing societies does not imply that the *same* values are not recognized by these different societies. According to him, there may be different norms while the *same* values are recognized. In Scheler's own words,

> *All imperatives* and *norms* can *vary* historically and with different groups, even when the *same values* are recognised; and they can continue to vary, even when the same propositions of the *ideal* ought are affirmed.[48]

Or, elsewhere,

> There may well be quite different laws or any number of laws of exception in the presence of the *same* moral values and the same order of ranks, but nothing can be said against the objectivity and identity of moral values because of this state of affairs.[49]

Thus, from the fact that different societies have different norms, it does *not* follow that values *themselves* differ in the sense of being given as "relative" to a given society. For, norms are not the ultimate facts of moral life as values are. It is rather the case that each society simply views these absolute values which are "autonomous facts" of moral life from its *own perspectives*, i.e., as if each is looking through a different window at the *same* absolute values. The relativity of norms to different ethos group does *not* in any way imply the relativity of values themselves.

Scheler observes that the different erroneous theories of historical and sociological variability and differences of values themselves have come into existence owing to either of the following reasons: (i) They clearly cannot distinguish the values themselves from their bearers, (ii) They fail to perceive and differentiate the fact that the changes occur only in the norms and *not* in the values themselves, (iii) They have not been able to recognize the objectivity and the positive insight into them. And finally, (iv) they are not able to see that values themselves are absolute as distinguished from the relativity of their judgement.

The historical relativity of ethical value-estimations and its different dimensions have got a sincere analysis in the hands of Scheler in his *Formalism in Ethics*[50] and other writings. One who is engaged in studying the historical moral facts, Scheler points out, he has to distinguish apart (i) the variations in moral value-estimation, (ii) the variations in "the stages of intellectual insight into outer and inner causal connections of things", and (iii) the variations in the techniques of action existing among different social groups. Now, in order to compare and analyse the relationship of different social groups to values themselves, it is necessary to reduce the social groups under analysis to the same level in terms of their intellectual culture, their technique of action, the levels of their value-judgements, etc. Scheler points to different complexities which lead different social groups to have variations and historical development of their ethical value-estimations. It is only necessary to remove all these complexities and disguises in order to discover the sphere of values, which is relative to each social group in their feelability and the problems with regard to the dimensions of the relativity of value-estimations. Scheler distinguishes five types of relativity which do not affect the realm of objective values and their objective order.

1. In the first place, the variations in the apprehensions of values themselves and therewith the structure of preferring values: Scheler calls it the variations in ethos. In this context, Scheler accuses ethical relativists, who believe that not only moral

value-judgements but also the values *themselves* are subject to historical development and change, of *not* recognizing the very historicity of the ethos itself. Scheler cites the example of the ethos of ancient Indian caste system which markedly differs from that of the Greeks. But these differences of ethos of the two different social groups do not in any way mean the relativity of values themselves, but only the relativity of the value-intuition which takes place in accordance with the ethos of each of the social groups. This *radical* type of relativity, according to Scheler, "consists in variations in the contents of an immediate value-consciousness and its governing rules of preferring."[51]

2. Secondly, in the context of variations in expressing our opinion regarding moral matters in judgemental and linguistic forms, Scheler distinguishes two types of ethics. One that contains our opinion in the form of naive beliefs with regard to ethical matters, and is practised by moral subjects of a certain age. This sort of ethics goes always with certain ethos. And the other represents "a relatively rare phenomenon", which is in the form of theories. This sort of ethics seeks to "justify" and also to "ground," in the highest of principles, the ethics of the former kind practiced by different social groups on the basis of the intuitive evidences of the ethos of its time. There are thus variations in these two distinct forms of ethics.

3. Thirdly, variations on the types of institutions, goods, and actions, which are founded upon some moral value-complexes: The examples of these types are marriage, murder, theft, etc. Theft presupposes the existence of property. But where the latter is not introduced the former cannot even occur. Or, the institution of marriage in its different forms (such as, polygamy, monogamy) must appear either as adultery or as legal behaviour.

4. Fourthly, there are variations in practical morality of people: That is, the evaluation of the factual comportment of people on the basis of the norms which belong to the order of ranks recognized by *these people* and which correspond to *their* own structure of the act of preferring. The practical comportment of these people can be evaluated by the ethos of *these* people only as the value of their comportment is completely relative to *their* prevailing *ethos*.

5. Finally, variations in the areas of *mores* and *customs* in which moral beliefs are expressed as distinguished from variations in practical moralities: These variations are in the forms of action and expression. The validity of these variations lies in the tradition of people.

Scheler's intention of considering the various kinds of variations at different levels is to say that none of these variations implies the relativity of moral values themselves. The above-mentioned variations do not alter the fact that "... values are irreducible, basic phenomena of emotive intuition."[52] Thus it is not norms but the values themselves that are pervasive and immutable in nature, and they remain so in spite of the variations that occur in different societies or races.

Evidently, there is *no* value-relativism but only the value-perspectivism that is involved here. "It is precisely a correctly understood *absolute ethics*," Scheler contends,

> that strictly *requires* these differences – this value-perspectivism of values among peoples and their times and this openness in the formative stages of the ethos. Because moral value-estimations and their systems are more manifold and richer in their qualities than the diversity of mere natural dispositions and realities of peoples would allow one reasonably to expect, one must assume an objective realm of values which our experiencing can enter only gradually and according to definite structures of the selection of values.[53]

6. Values as "higher" and "lower"

Let us now consider Scheler's discussion of the *hierarchical* order of values, which exists among values themselves. This order of ranks belongs to the very essence of values themselves as the difference between "positive" and "negative" values. This means that one value stands to another in the relation of "higher" and "lower". The order of ranks among values is totally independent of all kinds of historical and individual variability and is apprehended by us in special acts of value-cognition, which are called by Scheler the *acts of preferring*. Scheler says: "... the height of a value 'given,' by virtue of its essence, only *in* the act of preferring."[54] Thus Scheler points out that the height of a value is not "given" to us in the same manner as the values themselves are "given". As Schutz writes in clarifying Scheler's position,

> Preferring is an act of the emotional and intentional life on a higher level than the emotional functions by which the values are revealed. It is founded upon these functions of the lower level.[55]

To answer the question, what is meant by the act of preferring? Scheler carefully distinguishes *preferring* from *choosing*. First, an act of preferring is an act which provides us with the cognition of relations existing among values themselves, while that of choosing is always choosing between different deeds, and is an act of the will. Secondly, the act of preferring that takes place between values themselves is independent of the goods and is therefore *a priori*. But the choosing always presupposes the world of goods and deeds and is therefore *a posteriori*. Thirdly, according to Scheler, "'the height of a value' is 'given', not 'prior' to preferring, but *in* preferring."[56] And finally, it is not the precondition for the act of preferring that multiplicity of values be given in the feeling-acts to serve as the foundation of the former. On the contrary, the feeling-acts through which the values are given have their foundations by essential necessity in the "act of preferring" or "placing after". In other words, the values that are originally given to the acts of preferring can only be "felt" through feeling-acts. It must be noted that the rules of preferring are historically changeable, but the ordered ranks of values are themselves totally unchangeable and invariable.

Scheler then distinguishes *four* modalities of *a priori* order among values themselves starting from the lowest to the highest as follows:

1. The *first* order of rank consists of the values, which range from the agreeable to the disagreeable. They are revealed in sensible feelings. The values belonging to this order of rank are relative to the sensible nature, and not to any particular species, things, or events of the world which may be agreeable or disagreeable to organism. What is agreeable to one individual

may be disagreeable to another. But, according to Scheler, the preference of the value of the agreeable over the value of the disagreeable is absolute in nature; because, these values are given prior to any knowledge of things and events.

2. The *second* order of value-rank encompasses the opposition of the noble and the vulgar, or the good and the bad. These values are revealed by vital feelings. The correlative feeling-states of this value-rank are the feelings of health and sickness, the feelings of aging and oncoming death, etc. This order of rank, in Scheler's view, "form[s] an entirely *original* modality."[57] That is, it cannot be reduced to any other modes, and the failure to see the vital values as irreducible to any other mode is at the root of all erroneous theories ranging from Kant's formalism to utilitarianism.

3. The *third* order of rank is spiritual values which are given independently of the sphere of body and environment. These values are revealed by spiritual feeling and in the acts of spiritual preferring, loving and hating. The prominent spiritual values are (a) the aesthetic values of the beautiful and ugly, (b) the values of the right and wrong, (c) the values of the knowledge of truth etc. The correlative feeling-states of these values are, for example, the spiritual joy and sorrow, respect and disrespect, approval and disapproval.

4. The *final* order of value-rank includes the values of the holy and the unholy, which are exemplified in the objects belonging to the sphere of the absolute, independently of things, powers, persons, institutions, and the like, and which have been considered in various cultures at different periods as "holy". These values are revealed by "an act of a specific kind of *love,"*[58] which are essentially directed towards persons regardless of what "conception" of personhood is implied in a given era. That is, the highest value of the sphere of the holy is the value of the person. The feeling-states correlated with this class are ranging from blissful to despair, the faith and lack of faith, worship, etc.

The above orders of value-ranks have been expressed by Scheler in a close-fitting manner as follows:

> ... the modality of vital values is *higher* than that of the agreeable and the disagreeable; the modality of spiritual values is *higher* than that of vital values; the modality of the holy is *higher* than that of spiritual values.[59]

Let us now put together the various points that we have discussed in connection with Scheler's phenomenological theory of values. We may begin by pointing out that Scheler has clearly based the formulation of his value-ethics upon *his* understanding of phenomenology. At the first sight, what he values primarily in phenomenology is not a method but a peculiar *attitude* or a way of viewing. Adopting this attitude, one is able to approach directly the "things" themselves without all kinds of previous assumptions and thus one enters into an immediate relationship with "phenomena" themselves. In Seheler's value-theory, these "phenomena" are nothing but values or what he calls "value-facts". These value-facts are *pure,* in the sense that they are non-spatiotemporal and non-metaphysical *"existents"*. With these value-facts proceed the acts of the valuation, though the former are independent of the valuing man, his acts and the world of goods. All persons and goods presuppose values. Thus values are *a priori* facts of ideal nature in which all kinds of evaluative judgements, value-judgements, in particular, find their signification and fulfilments. "Ideal" nature of values precludes the possibility of their being posited. Secondly, concepts and propositions are inadequate for having a grasp of values. As they are pure *phenomena* or a kind of object, they are essentially incapable of definition; only concepts are definable. All kinds of symbols, signs or instructions are no help to get in touch with these basic "facts". They are given as pure "whatness" directly and immediately to essential intuition. Thirdly, a noteworthy aspect of Scheler's value-ethics is that he puts cognitive emotion at the centre of value-cognition; and thereby, he breaks down the age-old disjunction of reason and emotion. Scheler shows that there are a large number of feelings which have "objective" character and are actually a means of knowledge. He calls them "feeling of something" as distinguished from feeling-states. The former kind of feeling has intentional character which is capable of grasping its own kind of objects, that is, values, unlike the latter, which are mere psychological states of mind. According to Scheler, we get admittance into the objective realm of *a priori* values and attain the knowledge of them only in and through this cognitive function of intentional feeling. Fourthly, in Scheler's value-ethics, values are given an absolute, eternal and immutable status. And consequently, they are susceptible to change or variation, and therefore, in *no* way relative. He is quite aware of the fact that people in different societies practice diverse ethics; but *this*, according to Scheler, does not diminish or affect the absolute nature of values. Because what happens here is that the different societies "perceive" the *same* values from *different* perspectives, and accordingly, they form their own norms. It is due to diverse perspectival intuition of values, the norms vary and differ, while values remain the *same*. So, here, a "radical" relativity is involved in the sense that values themselves are not relative but only their perceptibility. And finally, Scheler discovers an order of rank among values as "higher" and "lower". There are such four value-ranks as belong to the very essence of values themselves and are revealed in a special act of cognition called "the act of preferring". These four value-modalities are: the values of the agreeable and disagreeable, vital values, spiritual values and sacred values.

Notes

1. Scheler, M. "Preface to the First Edition," *Formalism in Ethics,* op. cit. p. xix.
2. Scheler, M. "Phenomenology and the Theory of Cognition," in *Selected Philosophical Essays*, Translated by David Lachterman, (Northwestern University Press, Evanston, 1973), p. 137.
3. Scheler, M. "The Theory of Three Facts," in *Selected Philosophical Essays,* Translated by David Lachterman, (Northwestern University Press, Evanston, 1973), p. 215.
4. Ibid., p. 202.
5. Scheler, M. *Formalism in Ethics,* op. cit. p. 48.
6. Ibid.
7. Ibid.
8. Ibid., p. 49.
9. Ibid., p. 52.

10. Ibid., p. 49.
11. Ibid., p. 51.
12. Scheler, M. "The Theory of Three Facts" in *Selected Philosophical Essays,* op. cit. pp. 202-03, (our emphasis).
13. Scheler, M. *Formalism in Ethics,* op. cit. p. 51.
14. Schler, M. "Preface to the Second Edition," *Formalism in Ethics,* p. xxiii.
15. Schler, M. *Formalism in Ethics,* op. cit. p. 12.
16. Ibid., p. 253.
17. Ibid., p. 17.
18. Ibid., p. 18.
19. Ibid., p. 183.
20. Ibid., p. 166.
21. Ibid., p. 173.
22. Ibid., p. 167.
23. Ibid., p. 170.
24. Ibid., p. 174.
25. Ibid., p. 185.
26. Ibid., p. 23.
27. Ibid., p. 18.
28. Ibid., p. 19.
29. Ibid., p. 255.
30. Ibid., pp. 14-15.
31. Ibid., p. 176.
32. Ibid., p. 21.
33. Ibid.
34. Ibid., p. 20.
35. Scheler, M. "Preface to the Third Edition," *Formalism in Ethics,* op. cit. p. xxx.
36. Scheler, M. *Formalism in Ethics,* op. cit. p. 35.
37. Ibid., p. 255.
38. Ibid., p. 254.
39. Ibid., p. 255.
40. Ibid., p. 259.
41. Ibid., p. 258.
42. Ibid., p. 257.
43. Ibid., p. 258.
44. Ibid., p. 257.

45. Ibid., p. 259.
46. Scheler, M. *On the Eternal in Man,* Translated by Bernard Noble, (Student Christian Movement Press, 1960), p.184.
47. Husserl, E. *Logical Investigations*, Vol. I, p. 337-432, Translated by J.N. Findlay, (Routledge & Kegan Paul, London, 1970).
48. Scheler, M. *Formalism in Ethics,* op. cit. p. 215.
49. Ibid., p. 217.
50. Please see, Scheler's *Formalism in Ethics*, p. 299 onwards.
51. Ibid., p. 301.
52. Ibid., p. 265.
53. Ibid., pp. 303-4.
54. Ibid., p. 87.
55. Schutz, A. "Max Scheler's Epistemology and Ethics," *Collected Papers III,* op. cit. p. 167.
56. Scheler, M. *Formalism in Ethics*, op. cit. p. 88.
57. Ibid., p. 107.
58. Ibid., p. 109.
59. Ibid., p. 110.

7

Experiencing Values

We may begin by asking the question: *how* do we "experience" values? And this will be answered from phenomenological point of view. According to phenomenological ethicists, we do possess a cognitive phase in our emotional life that enables us to apprehend values. This cognitive-emotional phase is quite independent of psycho-physical organization as well as our rational faculty. In what follows, an attempt is made to lay bare the logic of the phenomena of the cognitive emotion *vis-à-vis* values apropos of Scheler and Hartmann.

The dichotomy between reason and sensibility, rationalism and emotionalism, has been playing a dominating role in most of the western philosophies from ancient times down to the present era. According to this dichotomy, reason or rationality is regarded as something lawful, orderly, logical, and as something superior to the sensibility or emotionalism which is considered to be unlawful, disorderly, and something which has no cognitive potential. Kant's philosophy serves as an eminent example where the above-mentioned dualism is found to be distinctly prominent. In his theory of knowledge, he speaks of two faculties, namely, "sensibility" and "understanding" from the joint operation of which knowledge arises. It is sensibility by means of which the representations of objects are given to us and understanding is a faculty by which we think or judge. In other words, "matter" of knowledge is supplied by sensibility, and the "form" is given by understanding. Here understanding has got a superior position, in the sense that it does not draw its laws (*a priori*) from Nature, rather prescribes them to it. Hence, "understanding makes Nature". He also identifies this contrast with what is aposterioristic and aprioristic. For him, that which is *a posteriori* is sensible and that which is *a priori* is thought or intellect. The similar trend is quite noticeable in his ethics. There he seeks to eradicate the sensible from his theory of ethics as he attempts to build it up on a non-empirical, non-sensible and *a priori* plane, which he calls "pure ethics" or "metaphysic of morals". So, according to him, it is Reason (and not human emotion) in its practical (moral) employment or function that guides our choices, i.e., what ought to be done or ought not to be done. For Kant, an action will have moral worth if it is done in conformity with the law of reason or the Categorical Imperative, without any influence or any role of inclinations or desires. Further, the ethical *a priori* must be *rational a priori* and can be expressed in judgements. Kant cannot conceive of the *a priori* that is *not* rational, namely, emotional. Because, for him, what is emotional is inferior to what is rational. Therefore, "... with Kant the intellectualism of the aprioristic is almost a settled principle."[1] Thus Kant denies any significant role to emotion as he accords to rationality in his moral theory.

Traditionally, in like manner, emotional contents of the mind such as, intuition, feeling, love or hate etc. are regarded as disorderly, and dependent on the psycho-physical organization of a person, and therefore they occupy a subordinate and inglorious position as compared to our rational faculty. But there are at least a few continental philosophers such as, Husserl, Scheler and Hartmann who put their arguments strongly against the view that everything in the human mind that is non-rational is dependent on man's subjective constitution and therefore cannot be our guide in our practical life. They show, on the contrary, that ethics can very well be based on emotions. That there are lawfulness, orderliness and cognitive capability of emotional life, which are differently irreducible to the lawfulness, orderliness of reason or rationality, has been paid due attention by these philosophers. By upholding this view, Husserl, Scheler and others break down the age-old rigid disjunction of reason and emotion. They show that there are quite a number of feelings, which have objective character, and actually yield knowledge.

We have referred to earlier that it was Blaise Pascal who with great emphasis said that "the heart has its reasons, which reason does not know."[2] Again, elsewhere he writes,

> We know truth, not only by the reason, but also by the heart, and it is in this last way that we know first principles; and reason, which has no part in it, tries in vain to impugn them.[3]

So, according to Pascal, our emotional life as a whole is not altogether chaotic or disorderly, but possesses the capability of knowing truth corresponding to that of our rational faculty. Later on, we find that Franz Brentano, one of the forerunners of phenomenological movement, recognizing the role of emotion in moral knowledge. For him, all mental phenomena including the emotional ones, unlike physical phenomena, are characterized by the fact that they are intentional[4] in character. Among these intentional acts, there are at least some such acts which are called acts of loving and acts of hating and which are capable of evoking a feeling favourably or disfavourably towards things or acts in their value-aspects. For Brentano, to say that an action is good or a thing is beautiful is to say simply that it is "correctly" loved. In his own words,

> We call a thing *good* when the love relating to it is correct. In the broadest sense of the term, the good is that which is worthy of love, that which can be loved with a love that is correct.[5]

Here the direct object of love is *not* the value itself but the goods or actions from which a value arises through the acts of loving.

This conception of Brentano is said to have given birth to both Husserl's and Scheler's view in this regard. For Husserl, "the heart and the will must have their analogous but specific forms of rationality."[6] And "values are ultimately experienced and given in value-feeling."[7] Scheler join forces with Husserl in this regard, and intensifies his personal insight by appealing to the analogous view of Pascal. He elaborates a theory of feeling in his major ethical work, namely, *Formalism in Ethics and Non-Formal Ethics of Values.* Scheler appears to have agreed with Brentano on a number of points with regard to the role of emotion in getting access to the world of values. Like Brentano, Scheler develops an intentional theory of the emotion and tries to elevate emotion to a place of prominence, which may stand on a par with our intellect to grasp objects, i.e., values. But he rejects Brentano's psychological interpretation of the emotive faculty. According to Scheler, Brentano has failed to see values as "facts" that are independent of our rational faculty, and also he has *not adequately* distinguished strict cognitive emotions from non-cognitive ones.

We should keep in mind Scheler's general standpoint according to which the division between the faculties of reason and feeling is a fanciful prejudice. "This prejudice," Scheler says,

> consists in upholding the division between "reason" and "sensibility", which is completely inadequate in terms of the structure of the spiritual. This division demands that we assign everything that is not rational – that is not order, law, and the like – to sensibility. Thus our *whole emotional life* – and, for most modern philosophers, our conative life as well, even love and hate – must be assigned to "sensibility." According to this division, *everything* in the mind which is alogical, e.g., intuition, feeling, striving, loving, hating, is dependent on man's *psychophysical organization.*[8]

As a consequence of this prejudice, ethics has always been formulated throughout history either as absolute, *a priori* and rational or as relative, *a posteriori* and emotional. Scheler regrets that ethics can be both absolute *and* emotional has seldom been given due attention. In order to build an ethics which is absolute yet emotional, Scheler endorses the Pascalian view that "... there is an eternal and absolute lawfulness of feeling, loving, and hating which is as absolute as that of pure logic, but which is not reducible to intellectual lawfulness"[9] and combines well with it some phenomenological insights.

He clearly distinguishes the kind of feeling which enables us to have the apprehension of values from mere psychological states of mind, the latter being non-cognitive in nature. Hartmann agrees with Scheler in recognizing that "the apriorism of thinking and judging is accompanied by an apriorism of feeling, the intellectual apriori by an emotional a priori which is equally independent and original,"[10] though he is avowedly a Platonic thinker. Let us now dwell on some of the details of the views of both Scheler and Hartmann with regard to the nature of emotional faculty that enables us to "see" values.

Let us first take up Scheler. According to him, emotional acts or what we have called feeling-acts are "feeling of something". This means that feeling-acts are intentional in character and their intentionality is directed towards some "objects" which Scheler calls "*genuinely* objective objects,"[11] to speak alternatingly, are values. This intentional relatedness between feeling-acts and their objects is *not* mediated by anything else like that of feeling-states which are purely psychological states of mind. In case of feeling-states, there may or may not have objects. If there is any object at all, the feeling-state becomes "related" with the former by way of objectifying acts, such as, of sensation, perception, thinking or representation. For example, a psychological state of mind, say, sadness, occurs in me due to my failure in the examination. Here there is "originally" no connection between sadness of my mind and my failure in the examination. It is only later, generally very quickly, I "relate" my psychological state of sadness with my failure in the examination through objectifying acts of "thinking". As Scheler points out, the sensible feeling-states, like sadness, do *not* have an *immediate* connection with the objects they intend. Therefore, my feeling of sadness has no "original" relatedness with its object, that is, my failure in the examination. Nothing *originally* is apprehended in the sadness. But in the case of intentional relatedness, as we have pointed out earlier, there is no such mediation of objectifying acts, and therefore, the latter is called by Scheler "original" relatedness. The intentionality of feeling-acts is *of itself* related to its object. Scheler says,

> For here we do not feel "about something"; we immediately feel *something,* i.e., a specific value-quality.[12]

Elsewhere, he points out that values are "... *facts of non-formal intuition, not* of sensible intuition, if by 'intuition' we mean immediacy of the givenness of an object ... ."[13] Further, feeling-acts are signifying acts, and are not dead and factual states of mind like feeling-states, in the sense that they *mean* some objects. That is, they are capable of providing us with the knowledge of some objects, that is, values. "That is", in the words of Roger Funk,

> feeling here reveals objects to me; it is neither a question of there being objects associated, either mechanically or through some mental act, with what I perceive nor of objects being brought in "from without" the experience, for feeling goes directly to *its* objects, viz., values.[14]

In other words, Scheler calls this feding a "goal-determined movement."[15] That is to say, it is the movement of emotional intentionality to bring some meaning into the focus of consciousness, to grasp a thing or an action in its *value*-aspect. This intentional feeling presents to us some mundane object or action with some spiritual meaning, that is, values. As Scheler says,

> ... this act plays the *disclosing* role in our value-comprehensions and that it is only this act which does so. This act is, as it were, a movement in whose execution ever *new* and *higher* values flash out, i.e., values that were wholly unknown to the being concerned.[16]

Furthermore, feeling-acts and its objects, i.e., values belong to the one and the same realm, that is, the immanent realm of moral consciousness. The feeling-acts, therefore, are related through intentionality to the objects of similar nature. The object does not lie outside the realm of knowing consciousness as in the case of feeling-states where the particular psychological state is aroused by outside cause. Hence, the process of value-experience is *immanent* to the emotional consciousness and involves no transcendent object. Thus Scheler says that "... feeling *originally* intends its *own* kind of objects, namely, '*values*'."[17]

The point to be added here is that for the involvement of values with the feeling, they themselves are not to be understood as "feelings" or "dispositions". Because, Scheler has given values the status of "objects" on the one hand, and specifies the kind of feeling through which they reach us, on the other. The latter has the cognitive capability apart from feeling-states. Hence, Scheler asserts,

> ... that values are given in a "feeling of something" does not imply that values exist *only* insofar as they are felt or can be felt. For it is a phenomenological fact that in feeling a value, the

> value is given as *distinct* from its being felt – and this is true in any *single* case of a feeling-function. For this reason the disappearance of this feeling does not cancel the being of this value.[18]

Having thus clearly distinguished the feeling-acts from the feeling-states, Scheler says that "values are given first of all in *feeling* (Fuehlen)."[19] They are given to us as intentional objects of our feeling-acts, as colours are given to us in and through visual perception. Values, according to Scheler, are completely inaccessible to reason, and hence, it is beyond the grasp of intellect. As Scheler writes,

> ... there is a type of experiencing whose "objects" are completely inaccessible to reason; reason is as blind to them as ears and hearing are blind to colors. It is a kind of experience that leads us to *genuinely* objective objects and the eternal order among them, i.e., to *values* and the order of ranks among them. And the order and laws contained in this experience are as exact and evident as those of logic and mathematics.[20]

In characterization of feeling-acts as the apt mode of value-cognition, one may trace here the phenomenological method of reduction. Husserl's concern to detach the sphere of intentional acts of knowing, believing, feeling, etc. from the psychological sphere of mind is shared by Scheler. Scheler's discovery of feeling-acts as a source of cognition is an effort in this direction, in the sense that he too, as we have seen, is concerned with distinguishing the feeling-*acts* from the feeling-*states*. Scheler also disengages value-essences from their bearers as also from *other* essences, which are given to intellectual perception. Now, by distinguishing the feeling-acts from psychological states of mind on the one hand, and by disengaging the value-essences from their bearers, on the other, Scheler seems to have found a *pure* cognitive level, leaving the world of specific objects on which values may "appear" under suspension. This cognitive level is "pure" in the sense that it is independent of the sphere of feeling-states as well as of the sphere of bare things. This is a reinterpretation of Husserl's theory of reduction by Scheler. We may justify this new interpretation on behalf of Scheler by putting forward the following considerations.

Our encounter with the natural world, according to Scheler, is infused by emotional grasping of values. That is, the world first presents itself to us as possessing certain values. For example, my apprehension of a given thing, such as, my table clock, would not have been possible unless I grasp beforehand the value of "usefulness" as I order my day's work, that is, how much time I shall spend in study, how much for doing physical exercise, etc. following this table clock. That is, the definition of table clock includes, among other things, the value of usefulness that is always pre-given. All our intellectual grasping of bare things follows later. In other words, in the order of possible givenness of objects, according to Scheler, value-qualities are given before everything that is value-free essences. All our intellectual apprehensions are founded upon the *affective* givenness of values. Because, it would not be possible to have the knowledge of what things are unless things are not given to consciousness as possessed of certain values. As Scheler says,

> A value precedes its object; it is the first "messenger" of its particular nature. An object may be vague and unclear while its value is already distinct and clear.[21]

Hence, Scheler holds that there is a primordial intuiting of value-essences, which serves as the logical basis of our perception of the natural world. The act in which we are opened to the natural world is emotional and takes place at primordial level when the meaning of accompanying perceptual act has yet not been grasped. At this level, human beings remain indifferent to the world of brute facts. That is, the latter remains under suspension. This is fundamental to the way, according to Scheler, men experience the world.

Now for Hartmann. The above analysis of cognitive emotional acts is quite acceptable to Hartmann as the latter has quoted the following from the writings of Scheler:

> Even the emotional aspect of the mind – feeling, preference, love, hate, volition – possesses an aprioristic character which it does not borrow from thought, and which ethics has to accept quite independently of logic. There is an inborn aprioristic ordre du Coeur, or logique du coeur, as Blaise Pascal happily expresses it.[22]

This "aprioristic character", according to Hartmann, is possessed by our emotional aspect of mind, that is, by what he calls "primal feeling of value"[23] or "primal consciousness of value"[24] and it is not borrowed from thought. The phrase "primal consciousness of value" means, for Hartmann, a primal and immediate capacity of knowing subject to appreciate the valuable. It is a matter of emotional *and* at the same time apriorical approval or disapproval, loving or hating for something, that is, values. Hartmann further paraphrases Scheler,

> Comprehension of ethical reality – whether it consist of goods, human relations or demands for a personal decision – is always, even for the naivest consciousness, transfused with valuations, with preferences in accordance with feeling, with strong tensions for and against. All acts which are related to this fulness of life and which grasp reality are at the same time acts which grasp values and which select according to values. But as such they are never purely cognitive acts; *they are acts of feeling – not intellectual but emotional.*[25]

Of one thing Hartmann is very clear. Values are known *not* through intellect; the latter has no role to play in the discovery of values. This is what marks them off from other objects of knowledge, which require the intervention of thought.

It is for Hartmann as for Scheler that these emotional acts are cognitive in nature having directedness towards their objects. As Hartmann, says,

> The grasping of them (i.e., values), however different it may be in other particulars, is just as much an act which goes out to something beyond itself as every other cognitive act ...[26]

In order to proceed towards further analysis of value-experience, a point that merits attention is the following. Phenomenological value-theorists like Husserl, Scheler and Hartmann want to defend ethics as a "pure" discipline as against moral psychologism and empiricism. That is to say, they are in favour of providing the ground for justification of *a priori* validity of values. Moral psychologism, on the other hand, is a doctrine which regards values and norms as the product of subjectivism, and seeks to make them relative to individuals or group; thereby the values and norms cannot be claimed to have universal validity. As John Drummond says,

> To ground ethics in psychology (or, similarly, in biology) would reduce moral laws to those empirical laws governing the activities of evaluating and acting rather than the universal and ideal laws governing the relations among the contents, i.e., the meanings, intentionally inherent in evaluating acts. To ground ethics in psychology would thereby undercut the possibility of any unconditional demand, of any adequate notion of obligation. Evaluative terms such as "good" and "bad" would refer exclusively to historically and culturally conditioned usages generally applicable only in particular times and cultures. They would have a merely factual validity."[27]

Now in order to avoid these consequences of ethics, the phenomenological value-ethics pleads for ethical absolutism. For the phenomenological thinker, the theoretical part of ethics must be *a priori* science and prescribe universal norms and commandments. So they are for grounding ethics on a level with universal validity. For them, values are absolute and subject to no change or mutation on the one hand, and the primary knowledge of them is not grounded on psychic subjectivity but rather on pure emotional subjectivity, on the other.

For the value-theorists belonging to phenomenological tradition, values are given, as we have pointed out earlier, through *emotion*. Here the term "emotion" is clearly not to be taken to mean "blind" drive, rather to mean *cognitive feeling* that has been elaborated earlier. The assignment of cognitive value to emotion is a deliberate step by Scheler in establishing a non-formal ethics of value. It is purely an "emotional contact" with the object, that is, values. This is "... in itself something unaccommodating, incapable of being disconcerted, a unique entity, a law unto itself, a distinctive orientation of values."[28] This is an immediate capacity to apprehend the values. No mediation such as, through concepts, symbols, signs, etc. are required in order to become aware of them. One is able to approach directly the "things" (i.e., values) themselves without any kind of previous assumption – be it naturalistic or metaphysical. He enters into an immediate relationship with the *value-phenomena* themselves. Thus Hartmann,

> Every moral preference is intuitive, is *immediately* there and is contained in the grasping of a given circumstance (whether it be a situation or a finished course of conduct). It does not first wait for a judgment of the understanding.[29]

For Scheler too, values are given *immediately,* that is, without the mediation of any kind of symbol, sign or instruction. This distinctive stress on direct, immediate and presuppositionless understanding of any phenomena is the hallmark of phenomenological approach to knowledge. Further, according to phenomenological value-theorists, the function of "pure" acts is not to be kept restricted to the domain of thought alone but to be extended to the domain of emotion as well. The emotional acts are in no way less "pure" than those of "pure thoughts". For, our emotional acts are totally independent of the psycho-physical structure of human beings like those of "pure thoughts". The *pure* acts which belong to our emotional sphere are totally different from feeling-states and they are not blind but cognitive in nature. Both Scheler and Hartmann emphatically claim the apriority of the emotional and severing of false unity that till now has existed between the *a priori* and the rational.

Thus far we have seen that the phenomenological tradition which goes back to the writings of Husserl succeeds in evolving and developing a methodology which is mainly oriented towards *non*-rational mode of cognition. Phenomenologists send out a message sharp and clear that it is only emotion and *not* reason which is the apt mode of grasping the value-phenomena. The rational means of cognition is neither immediate nor direct. For, reason cannot function unmediated by concepts, symbols, signs, etc. It is always seeking justification in terms of arguments based on deductive and inductive modes. Phenomenological value-cognition, on the contrary, is characterized by a mode of understanding, which is both direct *and* emotional-intuitive, and it needs no justification from outside.

It must be added by way of clarification that the emotional-intuitive acts are not contradictory to rational acts. Phenomenologists claim that both rational and emotional modes of cognition are different from each other, which have their respective autonomous area for itself. The logic of reason is blind to what we are given through the "logic of heart". As Spader points out,

> "... feeling" gives us an autonomous intentional access to the values (and their hierarchy) that are the bases for moral decisions.[30]

The emotional access to the realm of values is *not* vague or nascent and requires *no* subsequent clarification by reason as the order and laws contained in this experience are exact and evident such as those of logic and mathematics. Feeling-acts, therefore, are in no way aided by reason. And what these acts give us is in itself the basis of moral decision.

As the apprehension of values is an apprehension through emotion, one cannot shrink away from its object in order *not* to have the cognition of it. A valuing subject is *not* free to have or not to have the apprehension of values. Here he is purely receptive in matters of having the consciousness of values. The subject cannot keep himself aloof from the appeal made by value upon his "feeling". Rather, it is value-cognition that impinges itself upon one's consciousness. In the words of Hartmann,

> In this "beholding" of them the subject is purely receptive; he surrenders himself to them. He sees himself determined by the object, the self-existent value; but he himself, on his side, determines nothing.[31]

This point needs elaboration. According to phenomenological value-theorists, values are "materials" or contents and *not* concepts, symbols, or signs. They are something "original", "natural" and not something made, created, pre-designed or constructed through thinking. When a person encounters something valuable, he cannot but cognize such objects, that is, values. He cannot remain indifferent to it. Because, the value has a dormant power and energy of its own to determine the knowing subject. The subject remains passive in receiving the appeal made by value upon him. He is not free to accept or reject the appeal of value made upon him. For, the rejection itself would involve the apprehension of values. The subject is quite conscious that a value is enveloping him yet he is helpless to keep himself away from its cognition. *This* helplessness of the knowing subject to keep himself away from its cognition implies that this cognition is purely *emotional* in the sense elaborated above and it is, therefore, not at all grounded on reason or rationality. In case of such cognition, the knowing subject surrenders to values automatically and naturally to have the cognition of them. Thus values determine the subject and not *vice-versa*. Needless to mention, such determination is epistemological and may be termed epistemological determination. This epistemological determination does not, however, mean that the knowing subject would order his conduct accordingly. For example, one finds some money on a roadside without any claimant present there. He takes the money in his pocket intuiting fully well that taking of other's money without his permission is morally wrong. Thus, one's having the intuition of value does not in any way guide him to regulate any of his conducts. The point is that we are compulsorily *bound* to have the cognition of values but *not* bound to realize it in our conduct. And here lies the freedom of the person in moral sense of the term. Hence, persons are *not* free to have or not to have the cognition of values, but they are free to act according to his value-cognition or contrary to it.

It seems to be of great significance to discover in the emotional life of man an autonomous and orderly cognitive phase, if this is considered keeping in mind the whole philosophical tradition of the West. From Greek times down to the present era, reason or rationality has always been glorified as the only source of cognition and its apodictic certainty. And this seems to have culminated in Kant's philosophy which finds reason as the philosophical basis of our cognition as well as our conduct. As a consequence, human emotions such as love, hate, etc. are denied to be the legitimate sources of knowledge. Thus the phenomenological ethicists, like Scheler and Hartmann, discover an absolute and apodictic source of cognition in human emotion, which is in no way inferior to that of human reason or rationality.

The import of recognizing a cognitive phase in man's emotional life by Scheler and Hartmann can be better understood by situating the matter in the context of Kant's philosophy, particularly of Kant's ethics. Kant discovers his foundation of ethics strictly in reason or rationality, and the problem before him is to show as to how the moral judgement is to be legitimized. Because, for him, knowledge means judgemental knowledge. The moral law or the Categorical Imperative, for Kant, is the "fact of reason", and is judgemental in form and nature. One is able to judge the conduct of a person and can pass a moral judgement only on the basis of moral law. A conduct is judged to be good or bad on the basis of the conformity or disconformity of the conduct with the moral law, which is the law of reason. This means that Kant attempts to reduce values to moral laws in conformity with which a conduct becomes good. Phenomenological thinkers, particularly, Scheler accuses Kant of not being able to discover the fact of *moral insight* which is more original, fundamental and a definite source of moral judgement. For Scheler and other thinkers of this tradition, it is the moral insight or the intuition of values, which enables one to form a moral judgement on the conduct of a person. Moral judgements find their fulfillment in the pure intuition of values, which is pre-linguistic and pre-judgemental in nature. The logical category of truth and falsity cannot be ascribed to moral insight itself. Because, the latter is *alogical* in nature. This does not, however, mean that moral insight is something chaotic and disorderly. The moral insight referred to by the phenomenological ethicists has its own logic, order and regulation of its own. This is what they call "the logic of heart", which determines the truth and falsity of moral judgement and not *vice-versa*.

Let us now try to understand the importance of discovering cognitive aspect of man's emotionality by placing it against the backdrop of analytic tradition, that is, the meta-ethical tradition. The meta-ethical philosophers, as we are quite aware, are concerned with the meaning of value-concepts and value-judgements. Interestingly, these philosophers find the problem to lie in the *meaning* of moral concepts and judgements – as to what we mean when we pronounce a value-judgement. The task of ethical philosophy, for them, is only to determine the meaning of moral judgements, that is, to determine whether they are prescriptive, emotional, etc.

Scheler and other phenomenologists would view this effort of meta-ethical thinkers to find out the meaning of moral judgements through linguistic activity as meaningless. For, Scheler would clearly make a distinction between values as *contents* and values as *concepts*. The value-concept is a linguistic unit, which works within moral judgements and in a sense symbolic in nature. But what the phenomenologists call value-content is pre-linguistic or trans-linguistic and asymbolic phenomenon, and works among what is intended through feeling-acts. Here Scheler's point is that value-content and the value-concept belong to two *different* domains. The former "exists" as independent variable of emotional-eidetic intuition. But the latter "exists" as dependent variable as part of moral judgement. The value-concept is said to be dependent variable in the sense that after having grasped a value as content, one may call this intuited value-content as x, y, or z as he likes. These x, y, or z is the name or concept of values given to them by men. It may change from person to person or from time to time. But the value-content, which is termed as independent variable, remains the same. This distinction of value-content from mere concept clearly bifurcates the task of phenomenologist on the one hand, and the meta-ethical philosophers, on the other,

In concluding the above issue as to how we "experience" values, we summarize the main points as follows: Working within the phenomenological framework, both Scheler and Hartmann discover a centre of value-cognition in the "full-blooded" existential person. Both of them make an attempt to overcome the traditional dichotomy between reason and emotion, and establish emotional acts as a form of being aware of values. These ethical acts are *cognitive-emotional* acts having directness towards their objects, that is, values. These are the feeling-acts, which reveal the human acts or goods in their value-aspects and thereby they become cognitive acts corresponding to the cognitive acts of thought. Thus by the discovery of emotional *a priori* and the correlative domain of values, which address themselves to persons, Scheler and Hartmann establish the foundation of *non-formal* value-ethics as against Kant's formal ethics. And finally, we have considered these issues by situating them against the backdrop of Kantian and meta-ethical approach.

Notes

1. Hartmann, N. *Ethics*, Translated by Stanton Coit, (George Allen & Unwin Ltd., New York, 1958), Third Impression, p. 174.
2. Pascal, B. *Pensees*, in Robert Maynard Hutchins (ed.) *Great Books of the Western World*, Vol. 33, p. 222, (para 277).
3. Ibid., p. 223, (para 282).
4. Cf. Brentano, F. *The Origin of our knowledge of Right and Wrong*, Translated by Roderick M. Chisholm and Elizabeth H. Schneewind. Edited by Roderick M. Chisholm, (Routledge & Kegan Paul, London, 1969), p. 14.
5. Ibid., p. 18.
6. Melle, U. "Ethics in Husserl" in Lester Embree and Others (ed.) *Encyclopedia of Phenomenology*, (Kluwer Academic Publishers, Dordrecht, 1997), p. 181
7. Ibid.
8. Scheler, M. *Formalism in Ethics*. Translated by Manfred S. Frings and Roger L. Funk, (Northwestern University Press, Evanston, 1973), p. 253-54
9. Ibid., p. 254.
10. Hartmann, N. *Ethics*, op. cit. p. 177.
11. Scheler, M. *Formalism in Ethics*, op. cit. p. 255.
12. Ibid., p. 259.
13. Ibid., p. 166.
14. Funk, R.L. "Thought, Values, and Action" in *Max Scheler* (1874-1928): *Centennial Essays*, (Martinus Nijhoff, The Hague, 1974), p. 50.
15. Scheler, M. *Formalism in Ethics*, op. cit. p. 257.
16. Ibid., p. 261.
17. Ibid., p. 258.
18. Ibid., p. 244.
19. Ibid., p. 35.
20. Ibid., p. 255.
21. Ibid., p. 18.
22. As quoted by Hartmann in his *Ethics*, op. cit. p. 177.

23. Ibid., p. 178.
24. Ibid., p. 177.
25. Ibid., p. 176-77, (our emphases).
26. Ibid., p. 219.
27. Drummond, John J. "Moral Objectivity: Husserl's Sentiments of the Understanding," *Husserl Studies,* Vol. 12, No. 2, 1995, p. 166-67.
28. Hartmann, N. *Ethics,* op. cit. p. 86.
29. Ibid., p. 176, (our emphasis).
30. Spader, Peter H. "The Primacy of the Heart: Scheler's Challenge to Phenomenology," *Philosophy Today,* Vol. 29, No. 3/4, Fall 1985, p. 227.
31. Hartmann, N. *Ethics,* op. cit. p. 219.

8

Value-perspectivism: A Critique

We have already seen that both Hartmann and Scheler believe in the absolutism of values. Because, for them, values have their own kind of "reality" (for Hartmann, the mode of the being of values is like that of Platonic Ideas, and, for Scheler, values have the mode of "experience," or what he calls, "value-facts"). Values, according to them, do not depend on anything else for their existence; they are and subsist *independently* of anything else, and therefore, are self-subsistent. But this does not mean that they deny all relativism in the field of values and our experience of them. They in a certain sense, advocate relativism also in their respective theories of values. This absolutism-relativism antinomy in ethics stems from taking seriously two apparently conflicting yet equally important points. In fact, the relativism advocated by these thinkers, as we shall see, does *not* stand in contradiction with the absolutism of values. In other words, for both of them, axiological relativism does not imply the denial of what is value-absolutism. In order to see how these phenomenological thinkers become able to combine consistently two apparently contradictory positions, it would be worthwhile to explain the sense in which, according to them, values are *absolute* as also the sense in which values are *relative.*

Let us first turn to Hartmann's view. For Hartmann, values are "real" entities existing in a different world of their own *apart* from spatio-temporal world. They are "ideal beings" belonging to an ideal order, independently of all their bearers. They possess an independent and ideal mode of being like that of Plato's Ideas. Thus values, for Hartmann, have self-existence, though *this* self-existence is not real in spatio-temporal dimension and so is more appropriately called "*ideal*". This ideal being of values "exists" or rather subsists in itself independently of whatever else. Their peculiar mode of being is totally independent and therefore, they can*not* be *relative* to anything else. They are to be related to their bearers, i.e., persons and their acts; but this does not mean that they are relative to them. Values are eternal and not subject to any change or mutation. The independence and immutable nature is in no way affected by their relationality that they have with their bearers. *All this* means that in their mode of being, values are *absolute.*

Values, as we have already pointed out, are *a priori* for Hartmann. He takes the term *a priori* to mean both epistemological *a priori* and ontological *a priori*. Values are epistemologically *a priori* because they are presupposed in all phenomena of value-experience. They are *a priori* with respect to our experience of their bearers. They are the conditioning factors, which make their bearers valuable. On the other hand, in saying that values are ontologically *a priori*, what is meant is that in order for something valuable to exist, one must presuppose the "existence" of values. The "existence" of values conditions the possibility of something valuable to exist.

What needs to be stressed in the present context is the mode of their being *known.* Because *this* points to the way in which Hartmann accommodates the two apparently conflicting views first, that values are absolute and secondly that they are relative. According to Hartmann, it is through *emotion* that we can have the awareness of values. Here "emotion" is *not* to be taken in the sense of "blind" drive, but in the sense of *cognitive* emotion. We can have what he calls primary consciousness of values "which is an emotional and intuitive awareness of values in situations: personal and partial, yet (according to Hartmann) stubbornly truthful."[1] In order to get beyond the narrowness, partisanship and the unsystematic nature of the primary discovery of value, it is necessary to turn to intellectual reflections. This is the task of philosophical ethics which systematizes and orders our whole experience of values – both of our own and those of the other people.

Of these two kinds of awareness, that is, the *primary* awareness and *secondary* awareness, the former is more important for us in the present context. For, the former way of being aware of values is *phenomenological* in nature. It is an immediate way of getting access to the world of values. No mediation such as through concepts, symbols, signs, etc. is required in order to become aware of them. This is the first and "original" discovery. It is purely an "emotional contact" with the objects, that is, values. This is a primordial sensing of values, and an immediate capacity to appreciate the valuable. It is, for Hartmann, a non-logical form of comprehension, which is not transmutable into language or concepts. Thus Hartmann recognizes the role and legitimacy of "emotion" or "feeling" as fundamental to value-experience, which has its *own* order and lawfulness that are not borrowed from reason or rationality. Hartmann's founding of entire cognition of value-phenomena on the primacy of irreducible apprehension of values by "feeling" paves the way for him to advocate, as we shall see, a kind of relativism in a radical sense.

Turning to the question as to how the primary awareness of values takes place, Hartmann suggests that one should look into the deeper levels of moral life to find out the answer to this question. Every new conflict, every new expectation sets a new problem in human life and it is that which leads us to the primary discovery of values. Moral convictions of mankind change and differ. And this change and differing is *constantly* going on. In this process of differing and changing of ethos, every age, every society, every race, every generation takes part, and this differing and change can never be without value-orientation. It is in the context of the differing and change in ethos occurring among the societies and cultures that the primary discovery of values takes place. "In the revolution of the ethos", Hartmann says,

> the values themselves do not shift. Their nature is super-temporal, super-historical. But the consciousness of them shifts. From the whole realm it cuts out, for the time being, a little circle of something seen. And this little circle "wanders about" on the ideal plane of values. Every valuational structure, which enters the section of the seen and vanishes from it means for the evaluating consciousness a revaluation of life.[2]

To our understanding, the occurrence of "primary sensing" is always *perspectival* in the sense that every person, every society and every race "senses" values from a perspective that is relative to their knowing consciousness. What needs to be stressed at once is that far from rejecting value-absolutism which requires that all values be immutable and eternal beings inhabiting a Platonic realm of pure existence, Hartmann grants that discovery of some definite values by a society is *relative* to its perspective. In other words, for Hartmann, values as eternal, immutable beings belonging to an exclusive realm such that not all of them are accessible to any one individual or society at one point of time, but only some of them are accessible by intuitive means. It follows that different sets of values may be discovered by different societies; but this in no way should distract us from upholding value-absolutism. In elaborating this point, Cadwallader writes,

> ... insight into value-ideals is always essentially related to a particular "etheic" perspective by no means justifies philosophic subjectivism or even a rejection of Value Absolutism. Value-ideals, being platonic ideas, cannot *themselves* be relative to human cultures, or to individual human consciousness.[3]

In short, relativism is only with reference to "discovery" of values, even though values themselves are absolute. The "searchlight" metaphor provides the apt mode of understanding the absolutism of values, and also relativism with regard to their discovery. The perspectival focus of valuational consciousness of different persons, societies and races differ from one another. One perspectival feeling of values differs from the other, and therefore, they can never be the same. The object of primary sensing, i.e., the values, remain fixed, immutable and eternal. Corresponding to every perspectival intuition, there is a value or a set of values which is/are already "there" in the ideal plane.

The metaphor referred to earlier would bear some further reflection and elaboration, though we have already discussed it in an earlier chapter. Our value-consciousness is conceived of as a "searchlight" focusing across the field of values that are *static* and *immutable*. The searchlight of "primary sensing" "moves about" on the ideal plane of values and it exposes only one constellation of values at one time. Or, the focus of searchlight of different persons, societies and races may be thrown at different portions of the ideal value-plane *at the same time.* Now the focus of searchlight, i.e., of value-consciousness is thrown upon a relatively small portion of the vast field whereby the values are so apprehended. Though the ethical convictions of persons, societies and races change and differ, values themselves continues to remain static and immutable. For, "... values are independent of our differing and changing valuations."[4] But this does not, however, mean that we constantly add new values to the present stock of our intuited values. With new "unveiling" of fresh values by the value-consciousness, the concurrent "vanishing" or "forgetting" of other values takes place; that is, the values which at an earlier point of time have been in the focus of valuational consciousness, now shift away into the area of "darkness". And so, "... we always survey only a limited section of the realm of values, while we remain blind to the other sections."[5] Thus, in a manner of speaking, we might say that the actions, relationships, etc. which are regarded good today may be replaced by another set of values. What, however, is undeniable is that the values that are disclosed by any particular ethos-group appear as "absolute" to that ethos.

So far we have stated how Hartmann is able to maintain value-absolutism given his view that societies may opt for different value-schemes. The thrust of the matter is that values themselves do not differ or change in terms of their ideal content. What really changes is the *focus.* Out of an infinite value-ideals, one may discover only but a few or a small constellation of values. It is interesting to note that Hartmann argues for value-relativism if by that is meant changing societies adopting different values only on the ground and assumption that values themselves are absolute. Relativism of the kind referred to here can be upheld, Hartmann would argue, if only values themselves are taken to be absolute. What, then, is the nature of such relativism? Relativism, in a general sense, means that the values are relative to time and place, that is, relative to a particular society at a particular point of time. And any society may claim that its own standards are absolutely right and it condemns the standard of other societies Thus the standard of a particular society is valid for *that* society only and not for others. However, relativism in the present context may be understood in terms of the following: (a) that different societies/cultures seem to adopt or "discover" *different* values, and (b) that while the values are discovered, they are given as *absolute*. A point that at once emerges is this: that relativism, in this sense, does not destroy the objective validity and the consequent sanctity of values discovered by the societies/cultures. In other words, given a perspective, any society/culture would find or discover the same values. That it does not happen in point of history is because of the changing perspective.

Now, such perspectival intuition of values is termed as "value-perspectivism", which involves a kind of relativism in a radical sense. Because values themselves are not relative but the discovery and the continued discernment are relative, that is, relative to "ethos" of people at particular point of time and place. Hartmann thereby rejects the philosophical *subjectivism* which maintains that values are relative to individual human psychological constitution.

Thus it would seem to make sense to distinguish the kind of relativism that Hartmann advocates from the ordinary sense of the term. By rejecting both relativism in the ordinary sense and the subjectivist form of that position, Hartmann embraces relativism in a peculiar and unique sense, which may be termed as "perspectival relativism". In point of distinction, the relativism in this sense means that values are relative to a particular moral perspective. That is to say, values are relative to a particular perspective from which a particular individual, society or race establishes an "emotional contact" with certain constellation of values, and accordingly, they form their own norms and commandments. Thus there is a constellation of values corresponding to each perspective from which a person, society or race intuit the eternal and immutable group of values "existing" in an "objectively there" realm of values. This goes with Hartmann's position that different persons, societies or races experience values as "objective," existing in an independent ideal realm. Further, the perspectival "vision" corresponding to each constellation of values does not contradict other perspectival visions of values. It is possible for individuals belonging to one ethos-group to be aware of a quite different constellation of values from that which individuals of another ethos-group become aware. So, there are no conflicting value-apprehensions as there are only *differing* value-apprehensions. Cadwallader says,

> Thus it is entirely possible for persons of one ethos to apprehend (i.e., "perceive," "intuit," or "know") a quite different constellation of value-ideals from that which persons of another ethos apprehend. What would ordinarily be described as "conflicting" value-intuitions (in such cases) would then be more accurately described merely as *differing* value-intuitions. The psychological force of the searchlight analogy, therefore, is to enable one to conceive of a way in which mutually incompatible evaluations can be genuinely incompatible without necessarily being mutually contradictory.[6]

Further, values, according to Hartmann, are ontologically absolute and are multiple in numbers. Each value is absolute and each of them is caught in intuition as absolute by a perceiver who may belong to certain society or race. There are innumerable absolute values, of which a few only are grasped by a perceiver belonging to certain society or race at a particular point of time. In other words, no society or race is capable of intuiting the *whole* range of values *absolutely* but only a few. It is in *this* sense that value-intuition is perspectival. So it follows that relativism in this context has a bearing on the epistemological sense of grasping them and *not* on the ontological status of values themselves. That single value that is grasped in phenomenological intuition is done so in the absolute sense but depending on the ethos in which a perceiver is placed, only a few such values can be grasped at a time by a particular society or ethos-group.

Now to turn to *Scheler's view*. We may proceed by recapitulating his basic standpoint. Values have an *independent* mode of being, and are "phenomena" or essences in Husserlian sense and "given" to knowing consciousness. They are, in Scheler's term, phenomenological facts or what he calls "moral facts" or "value-facts". They are *a priori* to what can be given by inductive and particularly by causal knowledge. He rejects the subjectivists' claim that values as such, and moral values, in particular, are only subjective phenomena in man's mind, which do not have independent significance and existence. He argues that if values are simply the correlates of human acts of valuations, they would be variable and wholly relative. Moreover, in his phenomenological description of the nature of values, Scheler compares the mode of values with colour species by distinguishing them from individual colour shade. For him, values "exist" the way colour species exist. Moreover, values are "objects" much as the colour species are for Husserl. But they are *not* objects of sensuous intuition of any kind. They are "objects" of non-formal intuition, that is, of the intuition of a phenomenological kind and thus the values are intuitive *a priori.*

Here, a point that would be important to our understanding of Scheler's view of *a priori* intuition is that the traditional dichotomy between reason and emotion is not endorsed by Scheler. He shows that reason is incapable of providing us the methodological requirement to have the knowledge of values. Scheler legitimizes emotion rather than reason as a source of immediate necessary truths, that is, values. Value-facts are accessible only in this fashion through emotion and are grasped immediately and intuitively. Scheler attempts to lay bare a type of "feeling" possessed by human person which is far from being a "blind" drive, and they are actually a means of value-cognition. The crux of the matter is that according to Scheler, cognition of value is possible *not primarily* through intellect but is gained in and through *feeling* that is intentional and cognitive. He carefully distinguishes cognitive feelings from mere feeling-states that are capable of grasping their *own* kind of objects, i.e., values through their intentional acts.

This conception of valuational intuition leads Scheler to propose a unique theory of relativism in the field of values. Scheler recognizes, as we have noted earlier, the historical changeableness of norms and imperatives from one society to another, from one race to another. But this does not mean, for Scheler, that the same set of values is recognized by these societies or races. A society or race at a particular point of time intuits values according to the historical circumstance in which it is situated. Similarly, another society or race may intuit values from another perspective according to its historical situation. For example, in a preponderantly military society where war is a means of acquisition, the values such as courage, bravery, etc. are considered to be more useful for the general welfare than the values like industry, diligence, honesty, etc. which find acceptance in an industrial society. Thus, here, the two societies, (say, military society or the industrial society) intuit the eternal, immutable values from their respective perspective and obviously, their own perspectival "perception" would be different from each other. In a similar fashion, numerous societies or races "feel" certain values and prefer them each from its own standpoint which makes it possible for them to form their imperatives and norms accordingly. That is, in accordance with their respective *perspectival* "perception" of different values, different societies or races go to form their norms and imperatives to follow. The point is that the differences and variations in norms and imperatives are due to the perspectival differences among the societies or races. And Scheler considers that

> a correctly understood *absolute ethics* that strictly *requires* these differences – this value-perspectivism of values among peoples and their times and this openness in the formative stages of the ethos. Because moral value-estimations and their systems are more manifold and richer in their qualities than the diversity of mere natural dispositions and realities of peoples would allow one reasonably to expect, one must assume an objective realm of values which our experiencing can enter only gradually and according to definite structures of the selection of values.[7]

Besides, Scheler refers to variation in our opinions about moral matters. There are some opinions, which are mixed up with our prejudices; others are expressed in the form of ethical theories. But the differences of opinion regarding moral matters do not contest the fact that values are invariant and immutable. Further, there are variations in our social institutions such as, marriage, theft, etc. as also in the evaluation of practical conduct of men. Furthermore, there are variations in practical morality and in the areas of mores and customs. All these variations in no way imply the relativity of moral values when the matter is viewed from the standpoint of Scheler.

It is significant on the part of Scheler to recognize the historical variability of these different factors relating to any society or race or ethos-group as these are historical facts which one cannot change or alter. It is on these variable factors that the possible knowledge of value-essences depends. It is because of these changeable factors in different societies or races that the perspectival differences occur. That is, one perspectival intuition of values by an ethos-group differs from another due to these existing historical variations in ethics, moral institutions, etc. This implies that the *a priori* and indestructible realm of values depends, in certain sense, on the contingent historical changeability of historical situation where the knowing subject is placed, and this dependence is only *cognitive*. It is the historically changing factors that cause the variations in perspective and not the variation in values *themselves*. Because of one's placement in a particular historical situation, his intuitions differ perspectively from the other person who is similarly placed in *different* environmental situation. And this perspectival "perception" of values by an ethos-group is *relative* to *that* ethos-group only. These groups form their norms and imperatives in accordance with their perspectival "perception" of values. "It follows," Alfred Schutz summarizes,

> first, that at no time of its historical existence can any individual or group have a total knowledge of the realm of essences; second, that each perspective in which this realm is disclosed to each subject at any moment of its history is unique and irreplaceable; third, that only the cooperation of mankind, as a whole, of all coexisting individuals and groups and also of all succeeding ones which are unified by a common tradition, guarantees the growth of aprioristic eidetic knowledge.[8]

Now, our understanding the views of both Hartmann and Scheler regarding the absolutism-relativism antinomy shows that they tread similar paths to arrive at almost identical solution. The kind of relativism advocated by both of them does not contradict absolutism in ethics; rather, the former goes really to support and sustain the latter. Both Hartmann and Scheler recognize the perspectival intuition of values. That is to say, each society or ethos-group intuits values from its own perspective that has been formed as a result of being placed in a particular historical situation. This perspectival intuition differs from the perspectival intuition of another ethos-group or society on account of its own unique environmental situation. Or, it may be, that perceptival intuition of one generation may differ from another generation because of the difference of the times. And thus the values that are "perceived" or "felt" from a particular perspective may be said to be *relative* to that perspectival "perception." The emphasis is on the point that relativism, in this sense, does not affect the value-absolutism, as it is upheld by both Hartmann and Scheler. The kind of relativism advocated by Hartmann and Scheler has been termed by us as "perspectival relativism", which does not imply valuational relativity. For, values *themselves* are not affected by the perspectival intuition of persons or societies. They remain eternal, static and immutable despite the changes that occur in the norms and imperatives followed by diverse persons and societies. Thus relativism, in this radical sense, can go along with the absolutism of values.

The radical nature of this type of relativism can be made clearer if we compare it with its ordinary sense. The ordinary kind of relativism asserts that values are relative to time and place, i e., to particular society/ethos-group, and the latter may claim that its own standards are absolutely right. These types of relativism, which may be advocated by different societies/ethos-groups fundamentally, disagree with regard to values *themselves* and thus it imputes diversity in standards or values. Scheler writes,

> [The] value-relativism always rests on an absolutizing of value-estimations which depend on the idiosyncrasies and culture of the observer concerned. That is to say, it rests on the narrowness and blindness of the horizon of moral values, an outlook that is conditioned by a deficient sense of awe and humility vis-à-vis the realm of moral values and its expanse and fullness.[9]

But what we have referred to as "perspectival relativism" differs from the ordinary type in that in the former *no* such disagreement arises with regard to the values *themselves* as it is the case with the latter. It recognizes the eternity and immutability of values and it is only the case that different societies differ only in their *perspectival* "perception." Thus here there is disagreement in *perspectives* only, and *not* with regard to values *themselves.* It is their particular societal circumstances that lead their members to intuit a particular value or set of values, and this does not imply that they (the members of the society) would deny or condemn the values advocated by other societies. Thus values intuited perspectivally by each society are *relative* to that perspectival intuition only, unlike that of ordinary relativism in which values *themselves* are relative to that society.

A point that we should take note of is that the perspectival relativism pleads for a sense of "tolerance" at least in theoretical level in the sense that members of a particular society need not disagree and condemn the standard of other societies. The diversity in moral standards is quite a historical fact which none can change or alter. Recognizing the historicity of the diversity of standards or values "perceived" by different societies, one can transcend the conflicting levels of societal standards without condemning the standard of other society to prove its *own* standard to be absolutely right.

For a phenomenological understanding of values, in general and moral values, in particular, Hartmann's advocacy of value-absolutism is of crucial importance. In order to uphold this position, though Hartmann admittedly brings in the Platonic view of reality, the implicit logic of value-absolutism is tied up with objective validity of values themselves. The kind of relativism he resorts to can be distinguished from ordinary sense of it, insofar as the former and not the latter is adduced in support of the objective validity of values. By combining value-absolutism with what we have called perspectival relativism, Hartmann has rescued the realm of values from the pale of capricious subjectivism. One or other set of values is chosen or more appropriately "discovered" by people, not because of mere capricious preference, but because the values are "out there" objectively for the consciousness to discover them. Given a certain perspective, consciousness can but only discover values that it does and no other. Implicit in this is the argument that *anyone* from the same perspective (by virtue of being historically placed so) would always intuit the same values. This clearly goes for objectivity of values, which consciousness ensures by de-linking itself from pure subjective drives that are capricious in nature. The logic of the invariance of values is based on their absolutism. That is, the values themselves belong to an ideal domain which is independent of the historical events and flux.

Indeed a hardline phenomenologist would have reservation for subscribing to a view, which implicitly or otherwise presupposes any metaphysical or ontological commitments. Needless to mention, Hartmann's value-Platonism may be an easy target of criticism from a hardliner. But any phenomenological analysis would be sympathetic to the core idea that values themselves are invariant and provide the basis for the objectivity of value-judgements. Hartmann's value-Platonism is to be understood in this larger perspective. In order to invest values with invariance and objectivity, they must be held as belonging to an ideal realm, which transcends, and is independent of, whatever exists in space and time. His value-absolutism may be said to have an important underlined message, namely, that values "exist"; and that they do so in an ideal realm; for, if they did in space and time, they would not be invariant.

Of no less consequence is Hartmann's analysis which involves his accounting for and responding to the historical fact that different people/societies adopt different values which may give rise to the false impression that values are a mere matter of subjective preference and therefore, there is nothing objective about them. In order to obviate the latter difficulty, Hartmann explains the apparent change of values in terms of differing perspectives. Why an individual or a society adopts a value is because of the perspectives from which he/it focuses consciousness on the realm of values. Given his particular position/perspective, there is no other alternative but to intuit the values that he does. Hartmann's approach in this direction can very well be elaborated supportively by invoking the notion of intersubjectivity. As Cadwallader says, "Hartmann's relativism is *inter*-subjective."[10] To argue that an individual discovers a value relative to his perspective is also to claim that anyone *else* in his place would also discover the same values. The validity of values, therefore, can be upheld *intersubjectively* as one can sympathetically imagine different people discovering the *same* values, where they all view it from the same perspective. In a limited context, this is borne out even historically as a particular society may be known to apply generally the same norms of moral standards for judging the conduct of its own members.

Turning to Scheler, we also see that despite relativity of value-intuition, he claims objectivity for values on the ground held to be intersubjective. That is, for Scheler, value-perspectivism is of intersubjective in nature. As values are relative to the perspectival intuition of each society or race, whoever would "visualize" from the same perspective would also "perceive" the *same* value or set of values. A military society, to take our earlier example, where war is a means of acquisition may intuit such values as courage, bravery rather than, say, diligence, industry and honesty which are preferred intuitionally in an industrial society. Now, whoever enters either of these societies is compelled to have the "sensing" of respective set of values, i.e., courage, bravery, etc. or diligence, industry, honesty, etc. Thus values intuited by these societies are valid for each of them respectively, and there is no question of condemning of the values adopted by one society by another. In other words, whoever would come to "perceive" values from that societal perspective would "perceive" the *same* values which have been "perceived" by the military society or industrial society. Like Hartmann, Scheler advocates value-perspectivism which is intersubjective.

In conclusion, we may note that the idea of intersubjectivity, as we have seen, in the value-ethics of both Hartmann and Scheler is intertwined with the very phenomenological mode in which knowing consciousness grasps value-essences. Intersubjective basis for the validity of values is invoked by maintaining that a knowing consciousness from a certain perspectival position *must* always grasp the very same values as would be accessible to any consciousness from the *same* perspectival position. Thus the *fact* of differing "perception" of values does not affect value-absolutism which indeed may be taken as the implicit ground for holding the relativity of value-cognition.

Notes

1. Kraenzel, F. "Review of E.H. Cadwallader's book, *Searchlight on Values*," *The Journal of Philosophy*, Vol. 21, No. 3, August 1987, p. 242.
2. Hartmann, N. *Ethics*, Translated by Stanton Coit, (George Allen & Unwin Ltd., London, 1958), Third Impression, Vol. I, pp. 88-89.
3. Cadwallader, E.H. *Searchlight on Values*, (University Press of America, Lanham, 1984), p. 93.
4. Spiegelberg, H. *The Phenomenological Movement*, (Martinus Nijhoff, The Hague, 1971), Vol. I, p. 385.
5. Hartmann, N. *Ethics*, Vol. I, op. cit. p. 228.
6. Cadwallader, E.H. *Searchlight on Values*, op. cit. p. 95.
7. Scheler, M. *Formalism in Ethics*, Translated by Manfred S. Frings and Roger L. Funk, (Northwestern University Press, Evanston, 1973), pp. 303-4.
8. Schutz, A. "Max Scheler's Epistemology and Ethics," *Collected Papers III*, (Martinus Nijhoff, The Hague, 1975), pp. 171-72.
9. Scheler, M. *Formalism in Ethics*, op. cit. p. 304.
10. Cadwallader, E.H. *Searchlight on Values*, op. cit. p. 90.

9

Some Concluding Remarks

Since the advent of phenomenological philosophy, it has concerned itself mainly with philosophical methodology and epistemological issues. Though Husserl, the inaugurator of the phenomenological movement, is said to have dealt marginally with ethical issues and given a considerable direction to the subject, but the task of developing a full-fledged ethical theories within phenomenological framework had been the achievement of the kindred thinkers like Nicolai Hartmann, Max Scheler and others. Though Hartmann leans on Plato for his views on the ontological question of values, yet his debt to phenomenology cannot be ignored. The development of non-formal value-ethics as against Kantian formal ethics is clearly the result of the influence of phenomenology on his ethical thinking, though this phenomenology markedly differs from its original formulation. Scheler, formulates his ethical theory on the basis of Husserl's phenomenological programme without, however, looking for a glint of inspiration from Plato. Scheler's understanding of phenomenological method as applied in his value-ethics differs, in some respect, from Husserl's original version, and it is only because Scheler gives a new orientation to some of the phenomenological ideas to qualify them enough to deal with ethical issues.

1. After considering the cardinal principles of Husserl's phenomenological method to which both Hartmann and Scheler are indebted, we have shown, at our exploratory effort, some affinities of Moore's intuitionism with the way both these thinkers

develop the matrix of phenomenological understanding of values. The similarity that strikes us at the outset is that both Moore and the phenomenological thinkers alike put forward a radical critique of naturalism in ethics. Moore seems to believe that ethics must maintain an autonomy and sanctity of its own by *not* assimilating its objects to those of natural sciences. Good, for Moore, is a property of some natural object, but it is itself "non-natural." The nature of natural objects is descriptive while that of ethical objects are evaluative. And both of these objects have their distinct roles to play in our life. Unlike natural objects, the ethical predicates are used to evaluate human conduct, and guide us for doing this or that action as principles of life. Nothing of the natural world order is capable of playing this crucial role, that is, to provide a direction to our life. This spirit of Moore seems to be reflected in the writings of phenomenologists like Husserl and Scheler. Husserl develops a critique of *naturalism* in his theoretical as well as practical philosophy. He denies that the science of facts can provide the foundation for normative disciplines like ethics, axiology, etc. Similarly, Scheler rejects all ethics based on contingent goods and purposes, and credits Kant for the latter's rejection of such ethics. He clearly distinguishes values from goods and purposes, which are their bearers, and erects an ethics on non-empirical plane. The second point that merits our attention is that a sort of foundationalism has been advocated by both Moore and the phenomenological ethicists. For Moore, the primary question of ethics is: "What is good?" which entails the answer to the secondary question: "what ought I to do?" One has to intuit *first* what a good is for its own sake, and then only one is able to decide what action ought to be performed. The intuition of goodness is the *foundation* of moral decisions and judgements. Likewise, for Scheler, intuition of values is the *foundation* of all moral decisions and judgments, and hence of philosophical ethics. As Moore, Hartmann's concept of primary discovery of values is the foundation for what he calls the discovery at *second* hand, which is in the nature of value-judgements. Our third point is that as for Moore, good is an "object or idea", so for Scheler, values are "objects". Both Moore and Scheler reject the conceptual status of values, and hence their definability. Good can only be known by *non*-sensible intuition which seems to be somewhat akin to the intuition of phenomenological kind. And finally, both these thinkers have recourse to the analogy of values with colour to make us understand the simplicity, indefinability and immediate knowability of values. Just as one cannot describe the yellow colour but only can have the experience of yellow, so values cannot be described but can only be experienced.

2. One of the striking features of the value-ethics of Hartmann and Scheler is that both these thinkers radically call into question the dominant role of Kant in philosophy, in general and in ethics, in particular. They build a solidarity to develop non-formal or "material" ethics as against Kantian formal ethics. This, however, does not mean that the ethics, formulated under the influence of phenomenology, intends to be anti-Kantian. For, Hartmann and Scheler share many points with Kant on ethical issues, and they avowedly make concerted attempts to move beyond Kant's conclusions. It is in *this* perspective that their relation with Kant needs to be understood. Of course, one may trace here the significant role of phenomenology towards making a comprehensive critique of Kant's ethical views and in erecting an alternative edifice of ethics which stands poles apart from formal ethics.

Let us first turn to the gist of Hartmann's specific and pointed arguments against Kant's major ethical premises. Considering Kant as an exception to the historical perspective which regards values as concrete *a priori* essences, Hartmann criticizes Kant's "*subjectivism*" of practical reason. In Kant's ethical scheme, the authority of issuing of moral commandments vests with the *rational* will which is concerned with moral decisions. The rational will makes the moral choice according to its own laws and does not require a law from outside. And thus it is autonomous. But from Hartmann's point of view, the will cannot issue forth any commandment. The task of issuing commandments is entrusted to the objective values themselves. The will's inability to issue forth any commandment does not take away its autonomous character. For the autonomy of the will, according to Hartmann, consists in making decisions. Secondly, if the will is empowered to issue any commandments as regards the thing that ought to be, then the Ought would be subordinated to the volition. In other words, the Ought, as the objective reality, will be subordinated to *subjective* factors. This subjective principle will now set up the moral standard which cuts the very root of morality. Thirdly, the Kantian subjectivism makes it difficult to understand the freedom of the will. If the will sets up the moral standard, that is, issues the moral law, then how can it *transgress* that which itself is its product? On the other hand, if the will is not able to transgress the law, then it would not be a *free* will. Thus both autonomy *and* freedom cannot be claimed for the will. Fourthly, that the moral law or the Categorical Imperative is only a *formal* law of action has been criticized by Hartmann. In this context, he also rejects the Kantian view that the *a priori* is identical with the formal, and shows, on the contrary, that the *a priori* can very well be "material." Finally, Kant commits a great mistake, according to Hartmann, when he identifies the *a priori* with the rational and the *a posteriori* with the sensuous. For Kant, the ethical *a priori* can only be rational *a priori* and exists only in the form of a judgement. Hartmann's point is that the aprioristic knowledge is intuitive, though it is *expressed* in a judgment. The expression of the *a priori* in judgmental forms is only secondary and derivative; and it does not in any way affect our moral insight that we have in our moral life.

3. Now for some significant insights from Scheler's critique of Kantian formal ethics. In order to formulate a "material" ethics, Scheler seems to be under an obligation to refute the major premises of the formal ethics of which Kant's ethics is a paradigm expression. Despite his general agreement with Kant on several points, Scheler directs some pointed arguments against him. The central point of controversy between Kant and Scheler lies with their respective understanding of the notion of *a priori*. This crucial notion bifurcates the development of two kinds of ethics formulated respectively by Kant and Scheler. The "a priori" is taken by Kant to mean a *formal* law produced by a *rational* subject and this leads him to deny *a priori knowledge* of good and evil. And consequently one cannot pronounce any action to be good or

evil, but only according to law or contrary to it. In order to provide an unconditional foundation of ethics, Kant takes recourse to the *formal a priori* expressed in the form of a moral judgment of pure practical reason, leaving aside everything that is empirical or *sensible.* For Kant, our acts of will would be determined not by caprices, desires and inclinations but by *pure* reason in its practical use.

For Scheler, this is a total misunderstanding of the phenomena of willing. An act of will is not, in fact, guided by the law of reason as Kantian ethics proposes but by *values* themselves which are *a priori* "facts" or phenomena in the phenomenological sense. There is nothing like *a priori knowledge* in Kantian ethics but only formal a priori laws produced by rational subjectivity. Rejecting the Kantian *formal a priori,* Scheler provides an ethics based on *a priori* value-content of moral consciousness. In fact, the concept of Scheler's "material" *a priori* provides a character to ethics which is un-Kantian, or in other words, phenomenological. Hence the notion of *a priori* plays a significant role to turn upon an ethics that is "formal" to an ethics that is "material".

Secondly, as against Kantian formalism which takes the moral law or the Categorical Imperative as the basic fact of morality, Scheler takes values themselves to be the fundamental facts of moral life. This, in our view, is another significant point of departure for each other. Scheler argues that Kant has erred in locating the *original* source of morality, and so he reduces his ethics to imperativism. This original source of morality is discovered by Scheler in *values* themselves. Moral law or the Categorical Imperative originates from values rather than from human thinking as Kant conceives it to be. Unlike Kant, who employs high rhetoric for reason's capability to issue moral laws, Scheler finds a source of them in objective values to which moral consciousness has intimate emotional access. And it is values which provide a "solid" foundation to the moral law, and *not* Reason which fabricates them out of nothingness and expresses them in the pure form of judgement. The Kantian view that knowledge is the "construct" of the mind is unacceptable to Scheler. In fact, Scheler's effort to discover a source of moral laws in values rather than in Reason, as Ronald Perrin rightly points out, is far from diminishing the role of moral imperative, rather it can be viewed as the enrichment of moral domain.

Thirdly, Kantian ethics fails to appreciate the richness of our emotional life and the significant role it plays in morality. Scheler accuses Kant of not being able to recognize the fact that our primordial commerce with the world is emotional, and recognizes a pre-theoretical grasping of values by our emotional acts. In keeping with his mission to establish ethics on non-sensible plane, Kant misconceives, according to Scheler, the nature of our emotional life and displays a hedonistic conception of it. That is, for Kant, human beings naturally strive for nothing but pleasure, and they are bound to be determined by their natural inclinations. The only thing that is capable of determining the will is something beyond the domain of natural inclinations or emotions, that is, by the moral law issued by the pure practical reason. The feeling of respect, though non-sensible, yet it has no power to determine our acts of willing.

In Scheler's view, our emotional life is not a state of complete chaos of the pleasurable and painful sensations. It has its own order, lawfulness and cognitive competence which are not borrowed from "thought". Scheler denies the Kantian assumption that the rational order is the *only* order of knowledge. In fact, these two ways of experiencing upheld by Kant and Scheler in the sphere of morality is another major point which creates a chasm between formal and "material" ethics. Thus the significance of Scheler's critique of Kantianism, among other things, lies in liberating the ethical philosophy from stiff intellectualism and places it on a tender emotional level which has its own logic and rationality. And thereby it opens a new avenue for human knowledge.

4. Scheler's conception of "*material a priori*" referred to earlier bears some more reflections and elaborations. It is this key notion which enforces Scheler's arguments against Kantian formal ethics and works as the foundation for his "material" ethics of values. What Scheler calls "material" has been conceived by him in Kantian terms, that is, against the formal elements of experience. The title of his ethical work and every stage of the evolution of his conception of *material a priori* involve explicit reference to the

Kantian dichotomy of the formal and the material. Thus the emergence of the notion of the *material a priori* seems to be *contextual* in the sense that it is developed in relation to the context of Kantian formalism. But the origin of this notion lies in the phenomenological notion of *essence*. The essence is taken to mean "phenomena" in Husserlian sense as against the Kantian sense of the term. As a result, Scheler points out, the dichotomy between phenomena and noumena breaks down. Further, Kant identifies "materials" with the *sensible* manifolds given to empirical intuition in the universal form of space and time. They can*not* claim themselves to be knowledge. The "materials" in this sense are *not* independent phenomena but dependent ones. They are dependent on the faculty of understanding which bestows order and discipline upon them to construct a piece of knowledge. But in Scheler's conception, the materials mean the data of knowing consciousness that are given to *essential intuition*. Unlike that of Kant's, the "materials" are independent phenomena given to non-sensible intuition. They can claim themselves to be knowledge in their own right without subjecting themselves to the forms of understanding. The material, in this radical sense, neutralizes the Kantian bifurcation of the formal and the material. Once Scheler grants his theory of *material a priori* and identifies values with them, he can now argue that his ethics is founded on material values that are not only independent of contingent goods and purposes but provides a rigorous *a priori* foundation without succumbing to Kantian formalism.

5. Hence, phenomenological ethics is not the ethics based on contingent goods. For, with the latter, Seheler argues, any alteration in the realm of good would be accompanied by a change in the sense and meaning of good and evil. Nor is this kind of ethics founded upon the principles that are derived from *empirical* motives. It is also not based on contingent purposes which defines good and evil in terms of some purposes, and reduces values to the status of a technique to *achieve* certain good. Phenomenological ethics intends to be "pure" ethics that is purged of all empirical ingredients.

Phenomenological ethics remains integrated to the phenomenological ideal of presuppositionlessness. For it does not presuppose any truth of history, science, inherited beliefs or common sense regarding moral matters. A phenomenological ethicist like Scheler accepts nothing that is not immediately and clearly "seen", and thereby he wants to stand on his *own* reason. That is, such an ethicist seeks to found his knowledge claims upon non-sensible and non-intellectual intuition or in positive terms on "emotional" intuition. And the objects of such intuition are values. They are immediately and directly given to the knowing consciousness. Thus directing one's attention to *what* in fact is given to consciousness is the core of phenomenological ethics. No philosophical speculation or the metaphysical question of the ultimate nature of reality is to be raised at all. Phenomenological ethics seeks to eliminate all prejudices, all our taken-for-granted attitudes, etc.

The core idea of phenomenological approach is that it begins its investigation with the bare fact that something is given to consciousness and seeks to describe that "something." The latter is phenomenological "given" or what Scheler describes as the phenomenological "facts". In ethical context, these phenomenological facts are nothing but values themselves. An ethicist of this tradition begins his ethical enquiry with values as they are given to consciousness. So, for Scheler, values are "facts" of moral life and are distinguished from things, states-of-affairs, men, etc., that is, from their bearers. They are "pure phenomena" in phenomenological sense. For, they are disengaged from all kinds of sensory contents. Values are *foundational* facts of phenomenological description and it is on *this* basis that the edifice of phenomenological ethics is erected. It is the value-phenomena upon which phenomenology strive to redirect our philosophical attention.

6. It appears that phenomenology regards "experience" as the main philosophical theme, just as linguistic analysis regards language as the main focus of attention. Phenomenological philosophy is not primarily concerned with language but with a kind of experience. From phenomenological point of view, human beings do not use language as a ready-made tool for interpersonal communication, which is totally independent of his experiential

acts. For, meaning or signification lies not primarily with linguistic expression but in the noetic acts of consciousness. In our view, Scheler's moral epistemology too bears the same phenomenological spirit.

In general, language is the means for describing what we experience. Our encounter with essences or phenomena is also a kind of experience, which is "*emotional*". Scheler designates this encounter with values in consciousness as feeling-*acts* as distinguished from feeling-*states*. It is a kind of pre-theoretical, and hence, non-intellectual experience. This means that phenomenological intuition or experience is *pre*-linguistic. That is, this kind of experience takes place at a primordial level when language has not yet taken over its task of describing what is already experienced. This implies that language is posterior to phenomenological experience of essences. In fact, phenomenology seeks to explore the presupposition of language itself whose task is only to symbolize the items of experience. For Scheler, phenomenological philosophy is a "continual de-symbolization" of the world. It is language which symbolically represents the "things" that we experience. The human spirit knows only one thing, that is, essences which are given without being mediated by any symbol or sign. That is, they are self-given. The attention of a phenomenologist is directed towards what is self-given, that is, *prior* to language where the meaning or signification inherently waiting to be significant or meaningful. Concepts must get its fulfilment in conscious experiential acts. In abstraction from such experiential acts, the concepts will be devoid of meaning or signification. For the latter does not belong to concepts or to any linguistic unit but to the acts of phenomenological reflection. It is not meaningful to talk of concepts as if they existed *per se*. A concept cannot convey us anything or make us understand anything unless it is fulfilled in experiential acts. For the meanings or significations are not merely a kind of linguistic skill but presuppose certain *experiential* acts in which they find their fulfilment. In other words, any concept becomes intelligible only in the context of certain intuitive acts in which signification inherently persists. Hence it seems that the supreme task of phenomenology is to *disengage* human mind from language and to go back to the roots of language, that is, to the pure intentional acts. Any linguistic dispute or analysis presupposes *a priori* "seeing" in the mind's eye of what is said to fulfill the concepts. In short, language needs to be validated by our pure experiential acts in order to be meaningful. Herein lies the significance of phenomenological dictum "Back to things themselves". Thus it is on *this* basic approach that Scheler's moral epistemology is founded. The intentional *feeling*-acts of consciousness are a kind of signifying acts which are capable of providing us with some signification that are values unlike those of feeling-states that are merely the dead state of mind having no cognitive capability. This signification belongs to the feeling-acts themselves and not to the value-concepts which are posterior to such acts. The value-concepts owe their signification in the pure intentional acts of consciousness. It is only through the fulfilment of value-concepts in experiential acts that they acquire significance in man's moral life. The value-concepts *per se* do not harbour signification or value, though they are capable of representing what we encounter in pure primordial acts of intuition.

7. For Scheler as for Hartmann, values are apprehended through emotional acts of consciousness. Brentano and Pascal discovered a phase in man's emotional life which is capable of *grasping* value-essences. These cognitive phases are quite different from feeling-states. The feeling-*acts*, unlike feeling-*states*, are intentional acts, and the intentionality is directed towards values. This directedness of this cognitive act goes directly and immediately to their objects, that is, values. These acts are pre-theoretical having the capability of bringing some signification into consciousness. No instructions, signs, symbols, etc. are of any help to get in touch with them. The emotional consciousness grasps value as its *own* kind of reality, that is, as immanent object. This is, in our view, a *foundational* act in the sense that all judgments concerning goods and acts of person must "conform" to this act of consciousness in order to be in the *a priori* sense true. In fact, all philosophical ethics is possible only when the fact of essential intuition of values

is presupposed. It is on this primary discovery that the philosophical discovery or the discovery at second hand is dependent.

In another sense too, this intuitive act is *foundational.* This can be understood if we follow the fundamental way of our experiencing the world. The natural world appears to us always as valuational. That is, the things and beings of the world appeal to our mind as something *valuable* at a primordial level when our sense or intellect does not yet become functional. This act in which the values, as essences, are *"bodily"* given is *not* founded upon the sensible perception of valuable things. We may note here that Scheler holds quite the opposite view of Husserl, according to which, the intuition of essences presupposes the sense perception of the objects that embody the essences. Scheler's point is that from the perspective of the perceiver, this non-sensible value-revealing act takes place before all sensory or intellectual perceptions. Values are spontaneously revealed in the act of pure intuition without being conditioned by other kinds of acts – sensible, or intellectual.

8. The traditional antinomy of absolutism-relativism has received a unique and radical solution at the hands of both Hartmann and Scheler. The controversy between absolutists or relativists is that values or standards are either absolute or relative, but not both. Hartmann's key to the solution lies in his "searchlight" analogy. The searchlight of intuition is constantly in motion exposing now this, now that value or constellation of values. The fresh and new discovery of values necessarily involves "loosing" or "forgetting" of other values. And thus an action or relationship which was regarded as good yesterday may appear to be bad today. Thus the consciousness of values shifts, but *values do not.* This is quite acceptable to Scheler, though he does not believe in the existence of a "heavenly" world of values. For Scheler, values are perceptually relative to certain ethical perspective. Scheler, like Hartmann, recognizes the perspectival relativism of values but *not* relativity of values.

The variety of intuitionism that is advocated by both Hartmann and Scheler presupposes anti-subjectivism. In other words, the relativism adopted by Hartmann and Scheler is inter-subjective. This means that objective values are perceived by different societies or races from the perspectives of their own. And as a result, there would be no conflicting value-intuition but only *differing* apprehension of values. This inter-subjective apprehension of values provides epistemic objectivity to them.

Bibliography

Acton, H.H. *Kant's Moral Philosophy,* Macmillan Press, London, 1970.

Brentano, F. *The Origin of Our Knowledge of Right and Wrong*, Translated by Roderick M. Chisholm and Elizabeth H. Schneewind, Routledge & Kegan Paul, London, 1969.

Bharadwaja, V.K. *Naturalistic Ethical Theory*, Delhi University Press, Delhi, 1978.

Blosser, P. "Moral and Non-moral Values: A Problem in Scheler's Ethics," *Philosophy and Phenomenological Research*, Vol. XLIII, No. 1, September 1987.

Blosser, P. "Ethics in Scheler," in Lester Embree and others (ed.) *Encyclopedia of Phenomenology,* Kluwer Academic Publishers, Dordrecht, 1997.

Blosser, P. *Scheler's Critique of Kant's Ethics,* Ohio University Press Athens, 1995.

Bochenski, J.M. *The Methods of Contemporary Thought*, Translated from the German by Peter Caws, D. Reidel Publishing Company, Dordrecht, 1965.

Cadwallader, E.H. *Searchlight on Values: Nicolai Hartmann's Twentieth-Century Value Platonism*, University Press of America, Lanham, 1984.

— "The Continuing Relevance of Nicolai Hartmann's Theory of Value," *The Journal of Value Inquiry,* Vol. 18, No. 2, 1984.

— "Value Trichotomizing in Philosophy and Psychology: On Nicolai Hartmann and Karen Horney," *Philosophy and Phenomenological Research*, Vol. XXXIX, No. 2, December, 1978.

Cadwallader, E.H. and Eisenberg, P.D. "Platonism-*Proper* vs. *Property*-Platonism: On Moore and Hartmann," *Idealistic Studies*, No. 5, No. I, January, 1975.

Calhoun, C. and Solomon, R.C. (ed.) *What is an Emotion? Classic Readings in Philosophical Psychology,* Oxford University Press, New York, 1984.

Copleston, F. *A History of Philosophy*, Vol. VI, Search Press, London, 5th Impression, 1977.

Cobb-Stevens, R. "Being and Categorial Intuition," *Review of Metaphysics*, Vol. 44, September, 1990.

Crosby, J.F. "The individuality of Human Persons: A Study in the Ethical Personalism of Max Scheler," *Review of Metaphysics*, Vol. LII, No. I, Issue No. 205, September 1998.

Drummond, J.J. "Moral Objectivity: Husserl's Sentiments of the Understanding," *Husserl Studies,* Vol. 12, No. 2, 1995.

Drummond, J.J. & Embree, L. (ed.) *Phenomenological Approaches to Moral Philosophy*: *A Handbook,* Kluwer Academic Publishers, Dordrecht, 2002.

Emad, P. "The Great Themes of Scheler," *Philosophy Today*, Vol. 12, No. 1/4, Spring 1968.

Embree, L. and others (ed.) *Encyclopedia of Phenomenology*, Kluwer Academic Publishers, Dordrecht, 1997.

Farber, M. *The Aims of Phenomenology*, Harper Torch books, Harper & Row Publishers, New York, 1966.

— *Phenomenology and Existence: Towards a Philosophy within Nature*, Harper Torch books, Harper & Row Publishers, New York, 1967.

Findlay, J.N. *Axiological Ethics*, Macmillan & Co. Ltd, London, 1970.

Frings, M.S. (ed.) *Max Scheler* (1874–1928): *Centennial Essays*, Martinus Nijhoff, The Hague, 1974.

Frings, M.S. "The Background of Max Scheler's 1927 Reading of *Being and Time*: A Critique of a Critique Through Ethics," *Philosophy Today*, Vol. 36, No. 2/4, Summer 1992.

— "Max Scheler," in Lester Embree and others (ed.) *Encyclopedia of Phenomenology,* Kluwer Academic Publishers, Dordrecht, 1997.

Gadamer, H.G. *Hermeneutics, Religion and Ethics,* Translated by Joel Weinsheimer, Yale University Press, London, 1999.

Garnett, C. "Phenomenological Ethics and Self-Realization," *Ethics*, Vol. LIII, No. 3, April 1943.

Gupta, R.K. *Towards Purity of Morals*, Pragati Publications, Delhi, 1981.

Hartmann, K. *Studies in Foundational Philosophy*, Editions Rodopi, Elementa Series, Amsterdam, 1988.

Hartmann, N. *Ethics,* Vol. I & II, Translated by Stanton Coit, George Allen & Unwin Ltd., London, 4th Impression, 1967.

Hartmann, N. *The New Ways of Ontology*, Translated by Reinhard C. Kuhn, Henry Regnery Company, Chicago, 1953.

Hartmann, W. "Max Scheler's Theory of Person," *Philosophy Today*, Vol.12, No. 4/4, Winter 1968.

Hancock, R.N. *Twentieth Century Ethics*, Columbia University Press, 1974.

Husserl, E. *Ideas I: General Introduction to Pure Phenomenology*, Translated by W.R. Boyce Gibson, George Allen & Unwin Ltd., London, 5th impression, 1969.

— *The Idea of Phenomenology*, Translated by W.P. Alston and G. Nakhikian, Martinus Nijhoff, The Hague, 1964.

— *The Paris Lectures*, Translated by P. Koestenbaum, Second Edition, Third Impression, Martinus Nijhoff, The Hague, 1975.

— *Phenomenology and the Crisis of Philosophy*, Translated and an Introduction by Quentin Lauer, Harper Torch books, Harper & Row Publishers, New York, 1965.

— *Cartesian Meditations: An Introduction to Phenomenology*, Translated by Dorion Cairns, Martinus Nijhoff, The Hague, 1960.

— *Logical Investigations*, Vol. I & II, Translated by J.N. Findlay, Routledge & Kegan Paul, London, 1970.

— *Formal and Transcendental Logic*, Translated by Dorion Cairns, 2nd Printing, Martinus Nijhoff, The Hague, 1978.

Jordon, R.W. "Unnatural Kinds: Beyond Dignity and Price," *Man and World*, Vol. 20, 1987.

Joas, H. *The Genesis of Values*, Translated by Gregory Moore, Polity Press, Cambridge, 2000.

Kant, I. *Groundwork of the Metaphysic of Morals*. Translated & Analyzed by H.J. Paton, Harper Torch books, Harper & Row Publishers, New York, 1964.

— *Critique of Practical Reason and other Works on the Theory of Ethics,* Translated with a memoir of Kant by K. Abbott, Longmans, London, Reprinted 1954.

Kersten, F. *Phenomenological Method: Theory and Practice,* Kluwer Academic Publishers, Dordrecht, 1989.

Kraenzel, F. "Nicolai Hartmann's Doctrine of Ideal Values: An Examination," *The Journal of Value Inquiry*, Vol. 18, No. 2, 1984.

— "Review of E.H. Cadwallader's book, *Searchlight on Values: Nicolai Hartmann's Twentieth-Century Value Platonism", The Journal of Value Inquiry*, Vol. 21, No. 3, August 1987.

Kelly, E. "Revisiting Max Scheler's formalism in ethics: virtue-based ethics and moral rules in the non-formal ethics of value." *The Journal of Value Inquiry,* Vol. 31, 1997.

— *Max Scheler*, Twayne Publishers, Boston, 1977.

— *Structure and Diversity: Studies in the Phenomenological Philosophy of Max Scheler*, Kluwer Academic Publishers, Dordrecht, 1997.

Kearney, R. *Modern Movements in European Philosophy*, 2nd edition, Manchester University Press, Manchester, 1986.

Kurtz, P. "Phenomenology and Naturalism," *Journal of the History of Philosophy*, Vol. VII, 1969.

Liverziani, F. "Value-Ethics and Experience," A.T. Tymieniecka (ed.) *Analecta Husserliana,* Vol. XVI, D. Reidel Publishing Co., 1983.

Lohmar, D. "Husserl's Concept of Categorial Intuition," *EDMUND HUSSERL*: Critical Assessments of Leading Philosophers, Vol. III, Edited by Rudolf Bernet, Donn Welton and Gina Zavota, Routledge, London, 2005.

Luther, A.R. "Scheler's Order of Evidence and Metaphysical Experiencing," *Philosophy Today*, Vol. 23, No. 3/4, Fall 1979.

Landgrebe, L. "The phenomenological Concept of Experience." *Philosophy and Phenomenological Research,* Vol. XXXIV, 1973–74.

Mall, R.A. *Experience and Reason: The Phenomenology of Husserl and Its Relation to Hume's Philosophy*, Martinus Nijhoff, The Hague, 1973.

— "Husserl's Criticism of Kant's Theory of Knowledge," *The Journal of the Indian Academy of Philosophy,* Vol. VI, No. 1, May 1967.

Moore, G.E. *Principia Ethica*, Cambridge University Press, Paperback edition, London, 1965.

Moosa, I. "A Critical Examination of Scheler's Justification of the Existence of Values," *The Journal of Value Inquiry*, Vol. 25, 1991.

Moosa, I. "Are Values Independent Entities? Scheler's Discussion of the Relation between Values and Persons," *Journal of the British Society for Phenomenology*, Vol. 24, No. 3, 1993.

Mohanty, J.N. *Nicolai Hartmann and Alfred North Whitehead: A Study in Recent Platonism*, Progressive Publishers, Calcutta, 1957.

— *Phenomenology: Between Essentialism and Transcendental Philosophy*, Northwestern University Press, Evanston, 1997.

Moran, D. *Introduction to Phenomenology,* Routledge, London,2000.

Maitra, S.K. *A Critical Exposition of Nicolai Hartmann's Ethics*, Published by the author, Banaras Hindu University, Banaras, 1954.

Mackenzie, J.S. "Review of Nicolai Hartmann's *Ethics," Mind,* Vol. XLII, No.166, April 1933.

Nenon, T. "Willing and Acting in Husserl's Lectures on Ethics and Value Theory," *Man and World*, Vol. 24, 1990.

Owen, T.J. "Scheler's 'Emotive' Ethics," *Philosophy Today*, Vol. 12, No.1/4, Spring 1968.

Paul, G. (ed.) *The Cambridge Companion to Kant*, Cambridge University Press, Cambridge, 1992.

Paton, H.J. *The Categorical Imperative: A Study in Kant's Moral Philosophy,* Hutchinson & Co. (Publishers) Ltd., London, 7th Impression, 1970.

Prasad, R. *Karma, Causation and Retributive Morality: Conceptual Essays in Ethics and Meta-Ethics,* Indian Council of Philosophical Research in association with Munshiram Manoharlal Publishers (P) Ltd., New Delhi, 1989.

Perrin, R.F. "A Commentary on Max Scheler's Critique of the Kantian Ethic," *Journal of the History of Philosophy*, Vol. XII, No. 4, October 1974.

— *Max Scheler's Concept of the Person: An Ethics of Humanism*, Macmillan, Hong Kong, 1991.

Pleydell-Pearce, A.G. "Feelings, Values, and Judgements," *Journal of the British Society for Phenomenology,* Vol. 9, No. 3, October 1978.

— Review of Max Scheler's *Formalism in Ethics and Non-Formal Ethics of Values, Journal of the British Society for Phenomenology*, Vol. 7, No. 2, May 1976.

Pyka, M. "On Emotion and Self-determination in Max Scheler and Antoni Kepinski," A.T. Tymieniecka (ed.), *Analecta Hussertiana,* Kluwer Academic Publishers, Dordrecht, 2000.

Pascal, B. *Pensees* in *Great Books of the Western World*, Vol. 33, Edited by Robert Maynard Hutchins.

Pivcevic, E. (ed.) *Phenomenology and Philosophical Understanding,* Cambridge University Press, Cambridge, 1975.

Ross, D. *Kant's Ethical Theory,* Clarendon Press, Oxford, 1969.

Scheler, M. *Formalism in Ethics and Non-formal Ethics of Values: A New Attempt toward the Foundation of an Ethical Personalism,* Translated by Manfred S. Frings and Roger L. Funk, Northwestern University Press, Evanston, 1973.

— *Selected Philosophical Essays*, Translated by David Lachterman, Northwestern University Press, Evanston, 1973

— *The Nature of Sympathy*, Translated by Peter Heath, Routledge & Kegan Paul Ltd., London, 1954.

— "Towards a Stratification of the Emotional Life," Translated by Daniel O'Connor, in *Readings in Existential Phenomenology,* Edited by Nathaniel Lawrence and Daniel O' Connor, Prentice-Hall, Inc. Englewood Cliffs, 1967.

— *On Feeling, Knowing and Valuing: Selected Writings*, Edited and with an Introduction by Harold J, Bershady, The University of Chicago Press, Chicago, 1992.

— *On the Eternal in Man*, Translated by Bernard Noble, Students Christian Movement Press, 1960.

— *Person and Self-Value: Three Essays*, with an introduction, edited and partially translated by Manfred S. Frings, Martinus Nijhoff, Dordrecht, 1987.

Seebohn, T.M. & Kockelmans, J.J. (ed.) *Kant and Phenomenology*, Centre for Advanced Research in Phenomenology & University Press of America, Washington D.C., 1984.

Spiegelberg, H. *The Phenomenological Movement: A Historical Introduction,* Vol. I & II, Martinus Nijhoff, The Hague, 2nd Edition, 3rd Impression, 1971.

Schilipp, P.A. (ed.) *The Philosophy of G.E. Moore*, The Library of Living Philosophers, Vol. IV, Cambridge University Press, 3rd edition, 1968.

Staude, J.R. *Max Scheler: An Intellectual Portrait*, The Free Press, New York, 1967.

Schutz, A. "Max Scheler's Epistemology and Ethics," *Collected Papers III*, Martinus Nijhoff, The Hague, 1975.

Spader, P.H. "Scheler's Phenomenological Given," *Journal of the British Society for Phenomenology*, Vol. 9, No.3, October 1978.

— "The Facts of Max Scheler," *Philosophy Today*, Vol. 23, No. 3/4, Fall 1979.

— "The Primacy of the Heart: Scheler's Challenge to Phenomenology," *Philosophy Today* Vol. 29, No. 3/4, Fall 1985.

Shmueli, E. "The Universal Message of Husserl's Ethics: An Explication of Some Ethical Premises in Transcendental Phenomenology," A.T. Tymieniecka (ed.) *Analecta Husserliana,* Vol. XXII, D. Reidel Publishing Co., 1987.

Schlaretzki, W.E. "Ethics and Metaphysics in Hartmann," *Ethics,* Vol. LIV, 1943.

Sokolowski, R. *Introduction to Phenomenology*, Cambridge University Press, New York, 2000.

— "How to intuit an Essence," *Husserlian Meditations*: *How Words Present Things,* Northwestern University Press, Evanston, 1974.

Valori, P. "Phenomenology of Personalistics Morality," A.T. Tymieniecka (ed.) *Analecta Husserliana*, Vol. VI, D. Reidel Publishing Co., 1977.

Vacek, E. "Max Scheler's Anthropology," *Philosophy Today*, Vol. 23, No. 3/4, 1979.

Wyschogrod, E. & McKenny, G.P. (ed.) *The Ethical,* Blackwell Publishing Ltd., Oxford, 2003.

Index

absolutism, 87-88, 145, 149

acts of preferring, 121-23

actualized value, 76

Aristotle, 53

Bergson, H., 19

bracketing, 24

Brentano, 19, 130-31

categorical imperative the, 60, 62, 71, 129, 164

categorial intuition, 28-29, 113

Cohen, H., 16

Empirical Intuition, 60

epistemological *a priori,* 82, 146

epoche, 24

essence, 25, 60, 76, 166

essential intuiting, 102

Farber, M., 16, 21, 22

feeling-acts, 115-17, 132

formal *a priori,* 63

formalism, 53-54, 60-63

foundationalism, 33, 161

given, 56, 65, 67, 100, 104

Hume, D., 65, 66

ideal objects, 112-13

ideal self-existence, 81

intellectualism, 55-57, 71-73

intentional inexistence, 25

intentionality, 25, 103, 105

intersubjectivity, 157-58

intuitive identity, 100

Kant, I., 48-73, 128

Mall, R.A., 66

material *a priori,* 62
mental phenomena, 130
modus tollendo ponens, 52

Natorp, P., 16
natural fact, 100
naturalism, 34
naturalistic fallacy, 34-35
necessity, 68
noema, 25
noesis, 25

objectifying acts, 132
objective objects, 132
ought, 50

Pascal, B., 130
phenomena, 25-26
phenomenological fact, 100, 167
phenomenological intuition, 25-27, 39, 168
phenomenological reduction, 23-24
presuppositionless philosophy, 105, 167
primary sensing of value, 93

relationality, 88-90
relativism, 148-49, 155
rigorous science, 23

scientific fact, 100
searchlight analogy, 94, 148-49, 170
self-existence, 78-80
sensibility, 70, 128
subjectivism, 48-52, 162

tolerance, 156
transcendence, 26

understanding, 71, 128-29
universality, 69

value-objectivism, 43
value-facts, 60, 110